# Not
# Hearers
# Only

# Not Hearers Only

**A Practical Ministry
for Deaf People
in the Local Church**

Andrew Owen

THE WAKEMAN TRUST, LONDON

NOT HEARERS ONLY
© Andrew Owen 2007

THE WAKEMAN TRUST
(Wakeman Trust is a UK Registered Charity)
UK Registered Office
38 Walcot Square
London SE11 4TZ

USA Office
300 Artino Drive
Oberlin, OH 44074-1263

Website: www.wakemantrust.org


ISBN 978 1 870855 57 0


Cover design by the author, containing the sign 'Fellowship' from
*Signs of Life*, his dictionary of British Sign Language for use in
churches.

Printed by Stephens & George, Merthyr Tydfil, UK

# Not Hearers Only

## Contents

But be ye doers of the word,

and not hearers only,

deceiving your own selves.

James 1:22

# Introduction

One evening a meeting was convened by a town community association. It invited a fair cross-section of the community to discuss access for the residents to all the services in the town. A man in a wheelchair wanted to have ramps installed in key places. A working mum wanted later opening times. A blind man talked about being allowed to take his guide dog everywhere. An older lady spoke about needing more public benches and conveniences. The consultation ranged through a great many issues, notes were taken by the secretary, and people went home feeling their voices had been heard. One man remained. The secretary politely told the man the meeting had finished, but he stayed in his seat. He had heard nothing all evening – no one had considered that maybe a Deaf man would be there. That scenario happens all too often in a great many situations. But what about churches?

> There are a significant number of Deaf people in Britain, but very few go to church.

There are a significant number of Deaf people in Britain, but very few go to church. Some churches of different persuasions have welcomed Deaf people and are positively addressing their needs. Unfortunately, and it is a fact of life, conservative Nonconformist churches in Britain have failed Deaf people. That requires amplification. First of all, what are conservative Nonconformist churches? They are careful to follow the Bible in doctrine and practice. They are not charismatic and their worship does not borrow from the world. To some outsiders they are old-fashioned and formal. Such churches have not only failed Deaf people, they have *spectacularly* failed them.

For decades Deaf people in the community around such churches have lived and died unreached, many unaware of the true gospel. Deaf people are not welcome, because there is no access through language, communication, awareness or ministry in any way. That is why, sadly, the general view held among Deaf Christians in the UK is that such churches have failed Deaf people. The finger silently points, so the question must be asked – how have they failed them? The answer is in this book. This is an undisguised challenge to the conservative Nonconformist constituency, but a challenge that may be taken up and addressed.

This book has much practical help for a range of people:

1. Church leaders and members who are unaware of the needs of Deaf people in their neighbourhood.

2. Church leaders and members who want to bring Deaf people into church life, but don't know how to do so.

3. Those who are keen to be (or are at present) involved in specific ministry to Deaf people.

4. Those in the church who would like to have some personal involvement with Deaf or hard of hearing people.

5. Those who have a love for the gospel and a heart for reaching everyone in the community, including mainstream and marginalised groups, such as Deaf people, because everyone needs the gospel.

The fact is that many churches work hard to minister to a

range of marginalised groups – disabled people, wheelchair users, blind people, those with learning difficulties, elderly people, ethnic groups, and more. Ministering to such folk is good and proper, but much of that ministry is delivered verbally, because the recipients can hear. Deaf people are different from all these groups, not because of their physical deafness only – that is just one difference.

**The Saviour died for Deaf people also.** Being Deaf means a different way of thinking. It means a different culture, a different view of life. Deaf people are strangers in their own country, in their own community, in their own family. They are misunderstood and ignored and people are afraid of them. The church should not adopt the mindset of the world. The church should get involved, because Deaf people have precious souls just like hearing people. The Saviour died for Deaf people also.

Churches have a Scriptural duty to help Deaf people, but benevolence should not be the only aim. In fact in many ways it should not be an aim at all. Deaf people are people after all, with expectations and needs that should be addressed without presuppositions or misconceptions. Contrary to popular opinion, Deaf people have much to offer the church – the presence of Deaf people has the potential to enhance the church, speed forward its work of reaching others, and lead to much blessing.

Starting a ministry to include Deaf people brings many surprises. That is why many practical issues are dealt with in these pages, to provide help and advice when surprises occur. There are sensitive things discussed here that are not addressed elsewhere. This is no sanitised manual proposing the most reasonable view. Issues are addressed freely without influence from pressure groups – some are issues which Deaf and hearing people may feel uncomfortable with – and readers are left to form their own judgement. This is a personal journey born out of experience with a faint nod to 'political correctness.'

Views are strongly held in the Deaf community. Most of those views spring from hearing people's abuse and refusal to understand Deaf people's needs. There are many levels of abuse, some gratuitous and shocking. The bottom line is that Deaf people are neglected and abused through hearing people being unaware. There are strong views on one side, and there is blissful ignorance on the other. If this book were to tiptoe around, carefully avoiding strongly-held views, it would have no real value. No one would learn from the mistakes and pitfalls experienced by others, mistaken views would remain undiscussed and unchallenged, and there would be no smoothing of the way for others attempting the same journey.

**Deaf people are neglected and abused through hearing people being unaware.**

There are many churches unaware of these important issues. They are unaware that they have neglected the Deaf community for so long. Bringing this to their attention will by God's grace spark something off that will greatly benefit and bless many Deaf and hearing people in the community. May it be so for the Lord Jesus' sake.

# ONE

# Some Statistics

There are 8.7 million people living in the UK who are Deaf[1] or hard of hearing. That is one in seven of the population. A massive 6 million of those are aged 60 and above, and have lost their hearing as part of growing old.[2] Most of these will not know sign language or feel the need to learn.

Approximately 8.5 million people are hard of hearing. Many in that category will not regard themselves as Deaf, or want to associate with those who are part of what is most definitely a Deaf cultural minority, using sign language. Deaf people are a different group, with their own desires and needs.

The elderly lady cannot hear her grandchild. 'Wait till I get my glasses on,' she says, 'then I can hear you.' She has suffered from gradual loss of hearing over time, but will not admit that she is lipreading. Many people like that will not use hearing aids. For many the use of a hearing aid is an admission of a problem. Many who lose their hearing later in life will do anything to hide it, and will not admit to it, even when loved ones are shouting ever louder.

[1] For an explanation of the use of the capital 'D' see chapter 12, page 128: 'Use the Right Terms'.

[2] Unless stated otherwise statistics in this chapter are from 2006 (various sources).

By contrast, around 50,000 people in the UK use sign language. Sometimes you see a figure of 70,000, sometimes more – statistics are patchy. Whichever figure you choose it is still larger than all the Welsh speakers in the UK.

When Deaf people frequent a particular pub, word gets around and hundreds may turn up, just to be with each other, signing frantically together. The impression may be given that there are huge numbers of Deaf people. That is because they tend to congregate together, sometimes in large groups.

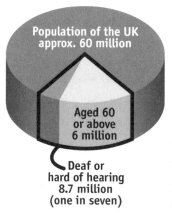

Hearing people rub shoulders with Deaf people more frequently than they think. You know a person is Deaf only when you attempt to communicate, or when you see two friends using sign language. You may pass people on the street every day, unaware that they are Deaf. Many sign language users regard it as their first language. Many of these were born Deaf or lost their hearing early in life. They are happy in their circle of friends and with the 'Deaf way'. They do not try to hide what they are as people.

## Which Group Are You In?

When we say someone is Deaf, what does it mean? Being Deaf is not just a physical thing, it is a cultural thing also. At the risk of pigeon-holing a huge section of society, we can attempt to classify deafness into four main groups:

**1. Hard of hearing people.** This is the biggest group. These people, the vast majority elderly, have a degree of hearing loss. Their first language is usually oral and written, such as English, and they usually identify themselves with hearing culture. Most will not learn sign language.

**2. Deafened people.** These people lose their hearing because of an accident or illness, some quite late in life. They usually identify themselves with the hearing community and hearing culture, although many deafened people feel lost between the two communities. Their identification with hearing or Deaf culture may depend on how early in life hearing was lost.

**3. Deaf people.** These people were born Deaf, or lost their hearing very early, sometimes before speech was fully developed. Such people will have sign language as their first language, and the national language as their second.

**4. Deafblind people.** In the UK there are around 23,000 Deafblind people of whom 15,000 are over 70 years old. There is a language for people who are both Deaf and blind. It is based on sign language, but is tactile. Communication with a Deafblind person involves holding hands while signing, and touching areas of the hand while fingerspelling (spelling out words with the fingers). For those who are Deaf and blind it is obviously extremely difficult to learn, and as so many Deafblind people are elderly, the difficulty is further compounded by the natural lack of enthusiasm for learning something new that comes with advancing age. A Deafblind person may use a walking stick painted red and white.

Although there are many people physically between the four generalised groups, a choice is made – Deaf or hearing? The plain truth is that there are two different worlds. Any ministry of the church needs to understand the difference. Hard of hearing and deafened people are hearing people with an auditory loss. Deaf people are different – they have a distinct culture, a different way of doing things, a particular way of communicating, a pride in who they are. Deaf people should not be regarded as disabled hearing people. In fact, most would strongly protest they are not disabled. If we are to reach Deaf people for the gospel it is essential we are aware of this.

There are many people who feel lost between the two worlds. To some their hearing loss is tragic. They suffer grief akin to bereavement. They lose their friends, and interaction with family is strained. Others are not worried about what they never had. They do not muse on the birds singing in the trees or the comfort of those little background sounds. Maybe sometimes they think it would be nice, though.

A Deaf friend was asked if she would accept an operation tomorrow that would give her full hearing. Without hesitating she said, 'No'. Her Deafhood is part of her as a person. She was nervous both about the operation and about having to change 'codes'.

## Children

Children have been left out of our four categories, simply because they may not have yet identified themselves with either the Deaf or hearing world, nor understood the issues. But children are important, and we need to consider them.

90% of Deaf children are born to hearing parents. Approximately three in every thousand children are born deaf. There are about 23,000 Deaf children under 16 living in the UK, so this category is very important. We will look in more detail at the importance of Deaf children and the church in chapters 10 and 11.

# TWO

# Culture

Are Deaf people the same as hearing people, but with a hearing loss? How do they perceive themselves? Is there still discrimination in the UK? Is an understanding of Deaf culture essential to understanding the Deaf community?

## Deaf Awareness

Imagine living in a community where no one understands you or can communicate with you, and where it is impossible for you to learn their language. So you live each day with your own thoughts. You can communicate by writing notes, but you are not too good at this because when you write you cannot use your first language. It is useful when you want to buy a bus ticket though, and you just about get by. There are other people who speak your language fluently, but you don't see them often, because there are few people like you, and they don't live near you anyway. So you seek them out whenever you can. You may never wander into a church, because how do you communicate there? Are there any people in the church who understand you? This is unlikely.

Deaf people have a 'way' of behaviour and living which is different from hearing people. They have their own society. To generalise, many do not enjoy communicating with hearing people (who understand little) and are at ease with Deaf people (who understand all). Deaf people live day to day in a community where few can communicate with them, and, with the exception of those who use lipreading, they cannot learn the 'hearing language'.

In the past a large number of Deaf children lived away from home in boarding schools, amongst other Deaf children. However, when they were back at home they would feel lonely, unable to communicate fully with their family, not knowing other local Deaf people. Strong ties would continue on leaving school, and Deaf people would travel great distances to meet old school friends, and large gatherings were very popular.

The desire to meet other Deaf people is very strong. As Deaf people are a minority, many cannot give full rein to social interaction during a normal day, and therefore seek out the company of other Deaf people, in clubs, pubs, etc. Integration with hearing people is not high on their agenda.

## The Deaf Club

There is a national network of Deaf clubs. These are social gatherings that exist to provide Deaf people with an environment where they can be accepted and feel at home. The Deaf club is where people can be with others of the same culture. Church missions and benevolent societies, many in the 19th century, traditionally set up these clubs. The Royal National Institute for Deaf people and the British Deaf Association owe their roots to similar initiatives. This is seen even today, because many such clubs are found in anterooms and basements of Anglican and Catholic churches.

Deaf clubs are found in many towns and villages. Some in rural areas open once a month. Some in the big cities open each evening. Membership is open to those who share the same physical, cultural and ideological characteristics. The strongest link is the language. The Deaf club is where Deaf people go to communicate with each other without inhibition.

The leaders of these clubs are not necessarily the oldest Deaf people or those most fit to lead, but rather those who subscribe most fully to the cultural ideology of the Deaf way. Some hearing people attend Deaf clubs, but they remain on the fringe. Some Deaf clubs do not allow hearing people. They are not a subversive resistance movement, although some hearing people may regard them as such. They are simply places where Deaf people can go and feel at ease. Deaf people travel great distances to attend these clubs.

Nowadays Deaf clubs are on the decline, especially in the big cities, because the younger Deaf generation are bored with sitting with the same old Deaf folk in the same old place. They seek out a more relaxed open environment, where Deaf people can just drop by and meet. In London, Deaf people congregate on a particular night at a particular place or area, by common knowledge. There is no membership or responsibility, and people come and go, signing frantically together. And the 'meeting place' can move inexplicably and without notice to another area. If you suddenly find yourself surrounded by numbers of people signing together in a park or railway station or cluster of restaurants, it may be you have stumbled on one of these 'mobile Deaf clubs'. People will be there from all over the place, because they know where their friends are and where to meet new Deaf folk.

If your church is known to hold a meeting especially for Deaf people, then those who are interested will come a long way to attend. It is important therefore to provide something to eat, and to offer an environment that does not force people into a hearing-structured meeting. Time must be given for communication and fellowship, more time than a hearing meeting usually offers. There will be more about this later.

## The Deaf Way

The 'Deaf way' is being honest with each other to the point of bluntness. It is wearing your heart on your sleeve, and using mannerisms which hearing people find comical. It is stopping in the street to sign to a Deaf stranger without inhibitions. It is not worrying about the passage of time. It is being open-hearted to children who are fascinated with the waving of hands. It is people bound together by similar experiences.

Traditionally, Deaf people are wary of hearing people, especially those who seek to communicate with them. A hearing person who uses British Sign Language (BSL) will not be regarded as credible without proof of BSL integrity. They will ask what level of exam has been achieved. Hearing people will sometimes experience the 'cold shoulder' in a Deaf club.

There is a BSL interpreter who is very good at her job. She moves in Deaf circles and works tirelessly for awareness and communication. Because she signs so well, some Deaf people at first think she is Deaf. Occasionally, when a Deaf person is told she is hearing, there is a sudden change in attitude and she is ostracised. The view is taken that she is somehow pretending or taking advantage, and they become very wary.

However, this attitude is not found everywhere, and it is changing. Deaf children are integrated into mainstream schools (there are strong views both for and against). Acceptance of Deaf people is improving, and BSL courses are popular.

## Discrimination

Deaf people are well aware of the cruel way they have been treated historically. Indeed, some who are older have lived through great intolerance, not only personally but against their language, which has been actively campaigned against. It is a sad fact that all Deaf people experience discrimination even now. Some believe that their culture and rights today are not recognised, and so behave in a radical way. Some Deaf people will use culture as an excuse. For example, Deaf people can be poor timekeepers (because time is such a vague concept) and may simply blame Deaf culture (this was pointed out to us by a Deaf friend).

Discrimination happens and is felt keenly, for example, when a less qualified colleague is promoted because of a perceived communication issue, or when hearing people do not try and communicate because, 'Well, Deaf people are used to not knowing what is happening anyway.' These things are disappointments, and should not be practised in our churches.

Some Christians may wonder why we are so concerned about a minority. They question the concept of doing so much for only one or two Deaf people. So much effort for so few. They can't spare anyone to help the one Deaf child in Sunday School, because there are many hearing children to look after, and all the helpers are so busy. The world holds a similar view, and Deaf people experience it often. Incidentally, the attendance of a Deaf child at Sunday School is a most precious and rare event, and a gift from the Lord, as we shall discuss later. A church that has been blessed with such a Deaf child must do all it can to provide support and understanding.

Remember the widow of Nain, in *Luke 7:11-15*. 'And it came to pass...that he went into a city called Nain; and many of his disciples went with him, and much people...' This is a favourite incident for preachers, who love to point out how far off the beaten track Nain was, and that the Lord Jesus took a huge detour because He knew that on the road outside that little, unimportant town a poor woman was in great distress. The Lord Jesus was going to raise a widow's only son back to life.

It seems He put His main objective on hold to seek out just one woman. He did it not only for the widow, but also as an example for us. His attention to detail and concern for individuals is demonstrated. For us, sometimes the most unexpected thing and the so-called 'lost cause' turns out to be a source of great blessing. Having a place for Deaf people in the church is only following the example of our Saviour.

## Reticence

Deaf people can be wary of entering a church that has many hearing people. Without any facilities for communication, a Deaf person will simply get nothing out of a church service. Picture a family from England looking for a church to worship in during their holiday in the hills of North Wales. The notice board is in Welsh, which probably means that the service is in Welsh also. The English tourists know that if they attend, there will be no understanding of hymns, readings or sermon. By the same token, a Deaf person will not walk into a church on a whim if facilities for Deaf people are not advertised. However, facilities for Deaf people are not enough. Friendliness and a willingness to communicate despite initial embarrassment will go a long way to counter reticence, and word will get round. The best thing to do, however, is to learn the language.

## Learning the Language

Those hearing people who have entered the Deaf world and begun to learn BSL are surprised and delighted with the richness and diversity of language and culture. Then, as they proceed, they begin to realise how dull their understanding was, how patient their Deaf friends are, and what needs to be changed, both personally and in the life of the church.

# THREE

# Communication

How do we communicate with Deaf people? Is it OK simply to pass notes back and forth? Are Deaf people happy for hearing people to learn sign language with the aim of communication? How long can it take to learn?

Most people are surprised to know that British Sign Language (BSL), as a language, was not officially recognised by the British government until 18th March 2003. Prior to that it was the subject of lobbying and pressure groups. Deaf people eagerly took to the streets and demonstrated to try to bring about change. The news of official approval came in largely unheralded in the shadow of the war in Iraq which began a few days later. Despite this political drawback, BSL was the chosen medium of everyday conversation for Deaf people, and, of course, continues to be so.

It seems ironic that prior to that date political conferences employed the services of BSL interpreters, yet the government did not allow recognition. Things are changing – the profile of BSL is rising. There are television programmes using BSL for Deaf viewers, and other programmes are repeated and interpreted later at night for Deaf people to record and watch at leisure. There are subtitling services on some channels.

Indeed, since the introduction of the Communications Act 2003, broadcasting access services for Deaf and hard of hearing people apply to all UK television broadcasters licensed by Ofcom. Local authorities offer an interpreter or a communicator for Deaf residents, and health authorities are increasingly seeing the need to communicate with Deaf patients. Although in many areas there is a great way yet to go, BSL is on the up.

## Fingerspelling Alphabet

At the foundation of BSL is the fingerspelling alphabet. If words do not exist as signs, then fingerspelling comes into play, being used for names, places, etc. Names and places are also given their own signs, so a person may have his or her own sign-name. These are based on physical features, mannerisms, etc. A person may have a sign-name without knowing it. For instance, a pastor may be sign-named by his church Deaf people, much the same as the headteacher is nicknamed at school. Most Deaf people have sign-names, because it's quicker than fingerspelling, easier to remember and friendlier.

BSL does not have a commonly known range of theological signs. Theological signs do exist, like jargon, but Deaf people unaccustomed to churches may not understand them. Explaining the precise meaning of terms in their Biblical language and theology can therefore be a minefield. Even with these drawbacks, BSL is the best means of interpreting church services for Deaf people, and an experienced and qualified interpreter can impart the essential meaning of the sermon and make everything clear.

Regional differences occur in BSL, just as local slang affects speech. Sometimes the signs are completely different. Signs for numbers, for example, differ around the UK.

## Where Does it Come From?

BSL, like the other world sign languages, is a language of Deaf people developed by Deaf people over the generations. It is not a language devised by hearing people, as some think. The documented history of sign language begins with Socrates (469-399 BC), but it was almost certainly around long before. The ancient Jewish *Talmud* mentions Deaf people using sign language.

How language itself came into being is the subject of much debate by those experts who take no account of the Biblical record of the origin of life.

## The Evolution Theory of Language

This debate came into popular thinking when Darwin's theory of evolution fractured a natural union and set science against the Bible. Sign language itself suddenly entered into the discussion and became something of a test case. One theory was that gestural language came first among human beings. This later developed into facial expressions and then into grunts and cries. Over time the noises changed and became words, and then were structured into sentences as intelligence developed. This theory ignores the fact that ancient languages were far more sophisticated than languages we have today. It is true that new words and concepts are invented constantly (such as 'internet' and 'gigabyte'), but we also know how common usage simplifies the complexities of language, even the very spelling of words.

The evolution theory of language was instrumental in forming a deplorable but popular view of the late 19th century, namely that the faculty of reason is linked to speech. It was held that Deaf people were not able to reason because they had no speech. Incredibly, this view survived until at least 1976, when *G W Hewes*, published by the New York Academy of Sciences, reported: 'The sign languages of the Deaf are dismissed as crude, rudimentary and if their users are unable to communicate except in such languages they display various serious cognitive handicaps.'

This is an example of how the evolution theory of origins has resulted in much vilification, cruelty and oppression, in stark contrast to the reconciling truth of the Biblical record, distilled in the gospel.

Unfortunately, although now no one dares to publish such sentiments, some people still hold that same unthinking attitude. They do not understand what is fact – Deaf people are as intellectually diverse as hearing people, but simply communicate in a different way. Deaf people regularly meet hearing people who yell at them, or treat them in an off-hand or downright rude way, as if their understanding itself were suspect.

## What is Makaton?

The Makaton vocabulary is a series of signs, which has been devised for the purpose of supporting the acquisition of speech for people with learning difficulties. It started as a research project in 1970, and has enjoyed wide acceptance in education. It has a vocabulary of signs but, unlike BSL, has no real grammar. It is sometimes described as BSL, but the only similarity is that it borrows some signs. It is more international than sign language, being used in over 40 countries. It can be of great benefit in the classroom (and home), because it is a communication link between student and tutor, so there is common ground for learning to take place. Its aim is to promote better spoken and written language. Many children and adults who are not Deaf, but have learning or speech difficulties, greatly benefit from this system.

## Is Sign Language Only British?

Other countries have their own sign language. American sign language (ASL), for instance, is different from BSL, and uses one-handed fingerspelling. It is used extensively in Africa (American missionaries exported it) and other countries. ASL has a bigger sign-for-word vocabulary than BSL, so in some ways it is more accurate. BSL users will say that their language is more expressive. The difference is often discussed.

An interesting event happened at a church meeting for Deaf people in England. A group of Japanese Deaf people was visiting (Japanese sign language is completely different to British sign language). A Deaf Japanese pastor was asked to address the meeting. His son was there, a Japanese sign language interpreter, who knew little spoken English. There was another pastor in their party, a hearing man who knew both spoken English and spoken Japanese. The interaction was as follows: when the Japanese Deaf pastor signed, the Japanese interpreter voiced into spoken Japanese; the hearing pastor then interpreted into spoken English; a British interpreter then signed into BSL for the British Deaf people. The story doesn't end there, because unfortunately some hearing people at the back of the meeting could not hear the spoken English interpretation, so a lady sitting with them who knew BSL voiced over from the BSL interpretation for their benefit. That meant that when the information reached their ears, it had gone through four separate interpretations. Also at the meeting was a Deaf man from Ghana. He did not understand BSL, so a member of the church (a Deaf man himself) interpreted from BSL into ASL, the sign language of Ghana. Interestingly, a hearing man in the meeting was taking notes, so he was asked for a copy of his notes for clarification. He replied it would be of no benefit to anyone, because he had written the notes in his native language, Romanian!

## Signs Only?

BSL relies on more than just the sign itself. The sign for 'Lord', according to one British sign language dictionary, has 15 or so other meanings, and the difference is in body language, lip shape, context and expression. For Deaf people a precise word such as 'conscience' (although known and understood by hearing people) is a specialised theological word, and is not generally known outside church circles in sign form. It may need a combination of signs to make the meaning clear, or it may require an explanation rather than simply fingerspelling. Some signs have to be invented, or explained some other way.

There are many words that do not have an equivalent sign. A simpler word must be chosen and signed instead. This means that a native BSL user may not have such a wide word vocabulary as some who have English as their first language. Many idioms which are used without thinking by hearing people, such as the cricketing analogy of being 'caught out', or the nautical phrase of 'nailing your colours to the mast', may be unintelligible to Deaf people. BSL is rich and fluent in other ways, and contains a wide expressive lexicon. Signs can be used in a positive or a negative sense, and some are almost impossible to put into words without using several words, sometimes a whole sentence.

Physically, the movement of signs is slow compared to speech. Words are said at roughly double the rate that signs are done, but it is possible to interpret from spoken to sign in the same space of time without losing any meaning. How is this possible? The answer is quite ingenious. Sign language relies less on 'words' and more on the intuitive use of movement and the three-dimensional use of space, location within that space, speed, direction, movement, the shape of the hands, all combined with information shown by the head, face and body. The eye can take all these things in at the same time. Many visual things can happen simultaneously, concentrating detail into the signs economically, so that the rate of ideas and subtleties of meaning fit within the time that speech is produced.

Academics have compared BSL with Old Testament Hebrew, because with Hebrew a great deal of information can be packed into a single word. Translation from Hebrew into English, therefore, involves unpacking that information. BSL crams a lot of information into signs, like Hebrew does with words. For instance, in BSL there are many 'classifiers', which are how the hands are shaped to show different meanings. One sign can be used to portray a person taking a walk. By altering the fingers, the sign can mean two people, or several people walking, or a child hopping. The sign can also include how the people are walking – in an orderly way behind each other or in a group – and the speed at which they are walking. The mood of the people can also be included. The single sign is packed with information. A BSL interpreter is therefore someone who packs and unpacks information.

**There is one sign which is the same in all the different sign languages around the world. It is the sign for the name 'Jesus'.**

## The Written Word

Many Deaf people do not understand the written word in the same way as hearing people. This is partly due to the fact that the early years are crucial in language acquisition, but people who are Deaf from early childhood are without hearing or speech to reinforce and practise English. Also, grammatical structure is different in BSL, so many do not have a full grasp of written language. It often depends on whether hearing is lost earlier or later in life, or on the method of education (more about this later).

It is possible to communicate by passing notes back and forth, but some Deaf people have only a scant understanding of written words. Because written grammar is different from the grammar of sign language, it is likely, when communicating in writing, for both parties to get hold of the wrong end of the stick. Hearing people will often rely on this method, and come away with the opposite view of what was meant. Sometimes, in an attempt to make the meaning clear, a hearing person will repeat a written question several times in different forms. This can be misconstrued. The repetition may be innocent because the written notes from the Deaf person were ambiguous. To the Deaf person, the notes were clear enough, and it may be perceived that repetition is being used to force a point home. Forcing a point is the last thing a hearing person should try to do to a Deaf person (as will be explained later).

> Forcing a point is the last thing a hearing person should try to do to a Deaf person.

## Should We Rely on Writing for Communication?

If a hearing person reads something written by a Deaf person, the temptation is to feel superior, because the language seems grammatically poor, badly spelt and childish. This is no reflection of intellect. When someone starts to learn sign language, the boot is firmly on the other foot. The signs are unclear, the grammar is confusing, and the person is slow, stiff and inexpressive.

Sometimes we see on television the head of state of a foreign country, an intelligent man, the leader of his country, but speaking in broken English. It is slow and unstructured, and wrong words are used. We are tempted to look down on him. But if he spoke in his first language and we could understand, then we would know how intelligent he was and form a different view.

The written word is useful, and sometimes is the only method available, but it should not be relied on. If you want to communicate fully with Deaf people then you must learn their language or, next best, find someone to interpret for you.

## Subtitles

When attempting to produce written subtitling for sermons, it is possible to produce near-complete reporting using a speech-to-text keyboard, sometimes called a Palantype machine. This is a sort of shorthand keyboard, which uses a system of sounds or 'chords' joined together, and phrases. The operator presses keys like a piano. A computer then turns the entered 'chords' back into English, and displays them on a computer screen, or projects them. The resulting text is usually 95% accurate, with a few words spelt roughly as they sound. A speech-to-text (STT) reporter can keep up with speech, but it requires some years training. STT reporters are members of a professional body.

During a sermon a good copy-typist can produce note-form text from speech, which is valuable, but editing of subject matter must occur (similar to when you take notes of a sermon to review later; your notes remind you of the details that were preached). Also the typist may miss points while concentrating on typing previous points. Many Deaf people will ask for a copy of sermon notes from the speaker, so that they can review what has been preached. Transcripts are like gold dust.

## Speech Recognition Technology

Software is constantly being developed which can emulate a human audio typist. The software 'hears' the spoken word and converts it into text. In the beginning of this technology, the software had to painstakingly 'learn' an individual's voice and 'guess' any words it had not learned. It was quite hit-and-miss, but now it is improving. Some subtitling organisations employ people who have 'trained' software to recognise their voice. They listen to the spoken message through earphones, and simultaneously speak the same words into a computer, but audibly adding, 'full stop', or 'comma', etc., so the software can construct sentences. We know of churches that have experimented with this technology for live sermons, displaying the text on a monitor.

This type of technology is good for those Deaf people who are able to understand the grammar of the written word, especially deafened people and those who can read well. There is a drawback, however – most Deaf people with little English, faced with the challenge of reading every word the preacher uses, will soon tire. The preacher will use phrases and words which will have no meaning to the Deaf person, because their first language is BSL. This impacts on Deaf people's grasp of Biblical wording. For a fuller discussion of this issue see the footnote on page 130. For those Deaf people who have sign language as their first language, BSL interpreting therefore is ideal.

## A God-Given Aid to Communication

'And Moses said unto the LORD, O my Lord, I am not eloquent, neither heretofore, nor since thou hast spoken unto thy servant: but I am slow of speech, and of a slow tongue...he shall be thy spokesman unto the people: and he shall be, even he shall be to thee instead of a mouth' *(Exodus 4:10, 16).*

Moses had an 'interpreter' – Aaron. God provided this essential aid to communication. Opinion is divided over the nature of Moses' problem. Was it stuttering or a pronunciation problem? Although God assured Moses that all would be well, Moses faltered and Aaron was provided. So started a partnership that was to last for many years. We should not be afraid of providing an aid to communication for someone who has a need. In fact, we have a duty to do so.

# FOUR

# Communication Through Drama

Deaf people express themselves visually. BSL is dynamic and expressive, so drama is naturally very much a part of Deaf culture. Deaf people love drama, so should we take advantage of that and use drama in church?

Some Christian Deaf clubs and churches use drama as a form of communication, and it is taught as a subject in Deaf institutions. We must be cautious, however, when linking drama with the church. As with all cultural ways and contemporary innovations, we must bring them into the clear light of Scripture. In the Bible preaching is the primary medium for communicating the truth of the gospel. We see in the New Testament the Saviour Himself, and people like John the Baptist, the disciples, the apostle Paul and others, exclusively using preaching as the means of proclaiming the gospel. Whenever the opportunity arose they preached to groups of people, whether they had gathered for the preaching or not – Paul on Mars Hill in Athens, for instance. We never see the apostle Paul resorting to dramatic presentations. Paul himself said in *1 Corinthians 9:16*, 'For necessity is laid upon me; yea, woe is unto me, if I preach not the gospel!' Drama is not part of the New Testament blueprint. It was preaching, preaching, preaching.

You may say, 'OK, but drama is not actually forbidden in the Bible. Can't we use a dynamic equivalent? Drama is a popular medium for Deaf people.' True, it is popular, but we must be careful and reasoned here. The gospel is the good news of sins forgiven. When it is presented in all its glory, it shows the justice of God throwing up a challenge to the sinful life, while the mercy of God presents a way of escape in the Lord Jesus Christ. So it contains many hard lessons to learn. Drama, however, is universally recognised as entertainment, and therefore inadequate and inappropriate for portraying a serious challenge to someone's lifestyle and character. People attending a drama expect to be entertained, and do not necessarily expect to be faced with the truth about their sin.

There is more: drama connects at an emotional level, particularly affecting the emotions rather than the will; it is associated with make-believe and dressing up. It stands or falls by the skills of the actors, and can only communicate a message, rather than give a direct challenge to the soul. It is easy for someone to view a drama at a detached level and go away spiritually untouched. It also draws attention to the actors. It becomes an art form in itself to be critically reviewed and applauded. Meanwhile the message, the important thing, is relegated to second or third place.

The real problems start, of course, when actors portray the character of Christ. Is the second commandment being broken? Also, drama is a medium that the world uses. There are some good, innocent shows, but there are also some filled with crude language, smutty double meanings, overt challenges to the standards of the Bible, and bad taste. Such shows are at the cutting edge of promoting all that the devil loves, and are constantly pushing at the barriers.

Traditionally, the church has been at variance with the theatre, and for good reason. Are we guilty of using the world's methods for God's work? His work is spiritual, not physical. The messenger must decrease and God must increase. He will honour the methods of His Word the Bible. Occasionally the Lord will work through other methods, but it will be in spite of rather than because of them. All these things make drama dubious at best.

Even the secular world recognises the distinction. At a political rally, speeches will be made. Later, in a lighter moment, a drama may be put on to entertain the delegates and poke fun at the other parties. There is a great contrast between drama and the preached Word. The best form of communicating the truth of the Bible for everyone, Deaf and hearing, is preaching using plain, old-fashioned proclamation.

You may say, 'OK, but what about using little drama-bites during a sermon to illustrate a point? No one will dress up.' Some churches today use this method, together with interjected readings, musical items, solos, etc., possibly because of the modern short attention span and the perceived need to have a happy, relaxed, enjoy-yourself environment, which will keep people coming. We should be very wary of trying to do God's work for Him. He is the One Who alone can change the heart and bring sinners to repentance. We should follow the pattern church, clearly blueprinted in the pages of the New Testament. We should worship Him in the way He wants us to and approach Him with reverence, because He is holy and His work is spiritual.

**We must allow the Bible to be our clear guide in all matters.**

This is not about imposing the hearing way onto Deaf people, indeed many hearing people love drama also. It may seem to some that nit-picking about drama is a futile exercise. However, we should identify the truth of what the Bible says, and apply it in our lives. We must allow the Bible to be our clear guide in all matters.

Drama is a very emotive issue with many Deaf people. A Deaf person reading this may feel a challenge to their culture and Deafness, and become quite upset. To propose the no-drama-in-church view in this book is a non-starter. Why? Because a hearing person is writing, and it strikes at the heart of Deaf culture. Be assured that the aim here is not to criticise culture or Deafness, but to follow God's Word as closely as possible. This clearly is the right aim. If we lay the patterns and formulas of the Bible aside, and do what we think is best and follow our culture, then there is no limit to how far we could go. It is a recipe for spiritual disaster.

Many Deaf people hold the no-drama-in-church view. The spoken word or signed message is clearly the best, and anyone who enjoys putting on a 'show' should consider the issues carefully. You may say, 'But you don't understand. Deaf people have a short attention span, because receiving information through the eye-gate is very tiring. You should provide something more visually stimulating.' That is true, so it is possible to break a long talk with a hymn or reading, or to use visual aids. We have had the experience of a Deaf man preaching using BSL for an hour and a half without a break. He used an overhead projector as a visual reference, and His Deaf congregation sat in rapt attention to the end.

## The Example of the Lord Jesus

We cannot open up the debate fully here, so careful consideration is urged. We should not make allowances because drama is a Deaf cultural thing. It most certainly is, but is it the New Testament way for making the gospel known? There are some cultural things that risk ruining the life of the church, and there are some that are actually against the Ten Commandments, and this may be one of them.

The Lord Jesus Himself had contact with Deaf people and we can learn much from how He approached them. His technique for communication and healing was identifiably modified, but never to the point of drama.

A Deaf man was healed in *Mark 7:32-35*. 'And they bring unto him one that was deaf, and had an impediment in his speech; and they beseech him to put his hand upon him. And he took him aside from the multitude, and put his fingers into his ears, and he spit, and touched his tongue; and looking up to heaven, he sighed, and saith unto him, EPHPHATHA, that is, Be opened. And straightway his ears were opened, and the string of his tongue was loosed, and he spake plain.'

The Saviour was here demonstrating His acute sympathy with the man's condition by healing him in a very visual way. When healing other people Christ would often confine Himself to speech only, but not here. The Lord Jesus was truly Deaf-aware.

Many people preach on this passage, offering various reasons why the Lord Jesus spat and touched, all of them good and reasonable. But we must look at the passage from a Deaf perspective. Only then can we begin to understand why the Lord Jesus did what He did. This was a practical visual aid designed for the Deaf man himself to understand.

The Lord Jesus took him aside from the multitude. He knew that Deaf people concentrate better with less visual 'interference'. Also if He were to deal with the man within view of the crowd, all the hearing people would stand and stare. Deaf people find that very uncomfortable, then and today.

Why did the Lord Jesus touch his ears, spit and touch his tongue? What was He doing? Consider the following: the Lord Jesus knows all the languages in the world. He gave Adam his speech. He confounded the builders of the Tower of Babel by giving them many different languages. The disciples were given many different tongues on the day of Pentecost. *Psalm 65:2* says, 'O thou that hearest prayer, unto thee shall all flesh come.' That verse means that anyone who prays anywhere in the world in any language is understood on high. *Daniel 7:14* speaks prophetically about the Messiah, the Lord Jesus Christ, 'And there was given him dominion and glory, and a kingdom, that all people, nations, and languages, should serve him.' The Lord Jesus is truly the supreme linguist. With that in mind, surely it is not fanciful to suggest that He knew Jewish sign language. In the absence of knowing what ancient Jewish sign language was like, could we not take one more step and suggest that in spitting and touching, the Lord Jesus was *using* Jewish sign language Himself? If you think that is too far-fetched, we could say that at the very least it was 'gesture'.

The Lord Jesus was doing four things. **Firstly,** by touching, etc., He was showing without speech that He knew exactly the man's need. **Secondly,** He was indicating visually the parts of the body where the healing was to be done. **Thirdly,** the Lord Jesus never healed anyone without his or her consent. It was essential that the Deaf man knew what was happening. **Fourthly,** the Lord touched because He knew that all Deaf people touch each other – to gain attention, and sometimes to make a point.

The Lord Jesus looked upward. Why? He was giving the man a good view for lipreading, without the deep shadows on His face from the strong Palestinian sun. He was also visually indicating from where the man's help came. He uttered only one word, 'EPHPHATHA' (be opened). One can imagine the clear way the Lord shaped His lips as He spoke, to give opportunity for lipreading. At that word the Lord Jesus healed the man and he was instantly able to hear. Clearly, He dealt with the man in a different way than He did when healing hearing people.

The Lord Jesus didn't stop there. The Bible tells us that the healing empowered the man to speak immediately. He was Deaf, but like most Deaf people, there was actually nothing wrong with the man's vocal equipment. The Lord Jesus performed two miracles, if you like: the Deaf man was made to hear, but the second miracle was that the Lord was short-circuiting the learning process needed for the man to hear speech and form his own sounds into speech. That learning process may have taken some time and practice, and the people who heard the man's faltering words may have been tempted to think that the healing was only half done. No; the Saviour's healing was always complete. By granting the man instant speech, the Lord Jesus was showing how aware He was of the man's condition and needs.

The Lord Jesus used many methods of communication: He taught and preached and told parables, His miracles were glorious visual aids, *but He never used drama.* We should be careful to follow His example precisely.

Consider Paul, that great apostle, missionary, God-inspired writer of many epistles of the New Testament, and God-ordained role model for the church in all ages. Paul wrote to the Philippian church under inspiration from God: 'Those things, which ye have both learned, and received, and heard, and seen in me, do: and the God of peace shall be with you' *(Philippians 4:9).* Paul was teaching them to follow his example. Paul never used drama. We should be careful to follow Paul in this also.

# FIVE

# Integration or Dedication?

**Do we at all costs integrate Deaf people into church activities, or do we rather have separate meetings dedicated for Deaf people? Are there ways that Deaf people can contribute spiritually or physically to the life of the church?**

There are two schools of thought. Do we encourage Deaf people into the 'hearing way' of worship, or do we provide an environment where Deaf people can worship with each other only? What are the differences? This is a big question of debate, and impacts on every area of worship. Hymn singing is a good example, and serves to highlight the issues.

## Hymn Singing with Deaf/Hearing Integration

Deaf people sing with their hands. As their language is visual-gestural, so is their singing. With that in mind, consider the following points.

1. Traditional hymns can have very difficult phrases and old-fashioned words, and their order is arranged to make lines rhyme. When an interpreter or a Deaf person leads singing, preparation is required to decide the most appropriate signs to use for difficult words, so that the meaning is clear.

2. When hymns are led, Deaf people watch the leader, and the words of the hymn, and sign together. Therefore it is not so easy to be aware of the whole line of a verse (scanned easily by hearing people). The words coming up, and the thrust of a verse are unknown, unless read through beforehand, or if it is a familiar hymn. A hymn projected onto a screen near the leader is ideal.

3. Without a hymn leader or projected words there are other issues. A Deaf person obviously cannot hold a hymnbook and sign easily at the same time. Synchronisation with hearing people suffers. Which verse is being sung? Tunes that require a repeat of the last line confuse the timing. Deaf people have finished, but hearing people are still singing. Or singing has stopped, but Deaf people are still on their feet. Either way it leads at best to fragmented worship. By contrast, hymn singing in a Deaf-only service is elegant and fulfilling. Hymns with more obvious wording can be chosen, traditional ones simplified, word meanings settled or words changed before the start. An overhead projector screen can be used and the place pointed out. Someone can lead the signing (as there can be different signs for the same word or concept). Everyone stays together and feels at ease. The hymn can be as slow or fast as the words demand because there is no reason to be constrained by a melody. Hearing people are often surprised at the beauty of a signed hymn, how understandable the signs are, and how Deaf people are able to worship with the same understanding, devotion, emotion and reverence as them.

## Deaf or Integrated Meetings?

Hearing people normally regard integration as the best solution. This view springs surely from a desire not to bar anyone from the life of the church. Also hearing people love to see Deaf people in church, singing and worshipping together.

When hearing people are Deaf-aware, and willing to provide adequate facilities, then Deaf and hearing alike are more at ease. For Deaf people though, integration is not the highest item on the agenda. It may seem obvious, but the best way to find out what Deaf people prefer in terms of integration is to ask them.

If we have a dedicated meeting for the ladies, the children, or a particular ethnic group, then we ought to have a meeting for the Deaf people of our neighbourhood. There may be many Deaf people living near your church building. Also, Deaf people will travel miles to meet together as part of their culture, so the challenge is obvious.

We must aim for both dedicated and integrated meetings. Deaf people have needs, such as to meet together as a minority where communication is complete, but hearing people must not bar them from taking a full part in the life of the church as well, both in worship and in service. The initiative is with the hearing people; but it is a hard pill to swallow, because the onus is on hearing people to change.

## Which Churches are Comfortable for Deaf People?

Deaf people are naturally drawn to contemporary Pentecostal and charismatic churches. There are two main reasons for this.

1. The worship of such churches is demonstrative and has an affinity with the physical nature of the language of Deaf people.

2. Such churches are open to change, and accept new ideas more readily. They therefore show a responsive flexibility when Deaf people start to attend.

Then there is the other end of the spectrum: the traditional, institutional church embodied in the Church of England, and the Roman Catholic Church. It is a fact that such churches in the past have oppressed groups such as Deaf people. Sometimes this has been unintentional, simply because their historical hierarchical structure has not been flexible enough to accommodate minority needs. However, speaking from a social perspective only, where acceptance has been attempted and achieved in a measure, these churches can offer comfort and security. But such security can also turn out to be very transient – we know of a church that was, at one time, very supportive of Deaf people, yet when the minister retired all that changed.

Practical love and acceptance are good aims, but they are not enough. The truth must be there, plus obedience to God's Word in personal lives and in the life of the church. There must be a framework of fundamental Biblical truth. That is unchangeable – because God does not change. We must not change our theology to find the best view to fit the Deaf case, although this is advocated by some (see chapter 8).

What about the old-fashioned, 'conservative' evangelical churches that have not been taken over by modern worship and charismatic practices? How many of these churches in Britain today have a ministry for Deaf people? They can be counted on the fingers of one hand. This may shock many people. Those churches want to keep to the pattern church of the New Testament, and are intent on keeping their worship reverent, and they doggedly reject each new fashion or trend that from time to time sweeps the churches and then fades away. That is all very good, but it means that when change has to come, for example to include Deaf people or any other minority group with their own needs, they are slow to take up the challenge. All too often Deaf people are left to find the church that accommodates them,

**All too often, Deaf people are left to find the church that accommodates them, rather than the church that holds fast to the Bible.**

rather than the church that holds fast to the Bible. This situation is not confined to churches – reformed conservative conferences, youth gatherings and holidays are closed to Deaf people also. We know of only one major reformed conference in Britain with access for Deaf people and sign language interpreters.

## What Changes Must be Made?

There are many far-reaching changes to be made. Perhaps the biggest change is in how people perceive deafness and Deaf people. Hearing people simply cannot fully understand what it is to be Deaf, not only in the church, but in everyday life. For instance, a Deaf lady is at home, but how does she know when there is someone at the front door? Or try this one, a Deaf motorist's car breaks down on the motorway. What does he do? He cannot use the emergency telephone because he cannot hear. Does he wait for the police to spot him, or for a passing breakdown vehicle? If so, he may have to wait several hours. Does he flag down a passing motorist?

Then there is the church service. Think about this scenario: a Deaf husband and wife arrive for the morning service, and the wife takes a seat while the husband visits the cloakroom. He comes out after the start of the meeting, and a prayer is under way. The husband cannot understand why the door is shut to him. He can see his wife through the glass. The steward explains that there is only a slight delay while the quiet atmosphere is maintained for the prayer, but the husband 'ignores' him and starts noisily pushing at the door. He is not ignoring the steward, of course, because he cannot hear the steward, but what should the steward do?

A Deaf husband and wife arrive for the morning service for the first time. He lipreads well, can use the induction loop system and wants to sit near the front to have a good view of the preacher. His wife wants to use the church interpreter, who is situated near the back. This means they cannot sit together like all the hearing couples in the congregation. You may think this is a small point, but for many people it is very important. There are many other such problems that will crop up when a church seeks to have integrated Deaf/hearing meetings. Who has the answer to all these things?

The answer is that changes need to be made. Just how much needs to be changed will remain a mystery unless and until hearing people pick up the gauntlet and positively address the issues. At the risk of leaving readers dissatisfied, we cannot provide guidelines and rules here, because every church situation is different. However, various practical suggestions are provided in chapter 12.

## Communication Link

If you want to provide an environment where Deaf and hearing people worship together, then an interpreter is vital. With an interpreter, the Deaf people will have access to all that is happening in a service of worship. Indeed, with a dedicated meeting for Deaf people, an interpreter is important also. Such a person can provide a voice-over for any hearing people who attend, and will enable hearing people from the church to preach from time to time. Deaf people can preach to the hearing also. We will look in detail at the role of the interpreter in chapter 7.

## Some Advice

In an integrated service where there is no interpreter, a hearing friend can stand next to a Deaf person, hold a hymn book and point to each word. Hands are free for signing, both know where they are, and can worship together. This is the same for the Bible reading. Simply telling a Deaf person the scripture reference is inadequate. The reference is announced, but not always where the reading ends. How does the Deaf person know when to stop?

There is something you can do, if it is acceptable to the Deaf person; point to each line and follow with the reader. Written notes of the sermon and also of the announcements and the prayer can be made so that the Deaf person can easily see them, but we must aim for better.

## The Prayer Meeting

Integrated prayer meetings are very difficult to orchestrate. In our traditional evangelical prayer meetings, hearing people have their own socially acceptable way of following each other in public prayer. If two people begin to pray at the same time, one will withdraw and allow the other to continue. The person who withdrew then prays next. Some churches have different methods, but when Deaf people are present, all too often they become observers. Why? There are many reasons:

1. A Deaf man would like to pray, but he has to rely on a signer. The signer may be nervous about voicing over from a signed prayer when all the hearing people are listening. It's a natural nervousness.

2. The signer may not be skilled enough to convey the prayer accurately, or the Deaf person praying is a man, and may not want his prayer to be voiced over by a woman signer.

3. In an integrated prayer meeting, a Deaf person starts to pray and the signer voices the prayer. The Deaf person cannot hear if another person begins to pray at the same time, so continues, eyes closed. The signer will have to steamroller the other person and win the battle to continue.

4. When a Deaf person signs a prayer, there may be short silences while the signer is receiving information, preparing to voice over. People may misinterpret the silence and think the

prayer has finished, voice an 'Amen' and wait for someone else to start a new prayer.

5. Loop systems are ineffective. Different people pray in various parts of the room, without stepping up to the microphone. The loop system cannot pick up any voice signal, so hard of hearing people cannot hear any of the prayers at all.

There are many reasons why it may be uncomfortable for Deaf attenders at a hearing prayer meeting. Constant frustration means that Deaf people will not attend. If this situation is to be addressed, changes must take place. One solution is that a separate prayer meeting is held for the Deaf people, and an interpreter is provided in case they want to attend the hearing prayer meeting.

## The Beauty of Integration

There is a certain beauty in an integrated church where Deaf and hearing worship together with parity. The hearing people thrill to see Deaf people singing. The Deaf people feel a part of the church, not bundled into the corner or sidelined like they so often are in the world. There is interaction and fellowship. People feel at home together.

There is opportunity to serve the Lord together. Integration is not something that happens in the meeting place only. Did you know that Deaf people can teach in Sunday School? They can pray, give out tracts and leaflets, and make up visual aids. They can drive, cook, offer hospitality, steward their money and serve as church officers. There are pastors who are Deaf. In fact there is very little that they cannot do, except hear.

Which is better: a hearing church member who is seen at only one meeting a week and never offers to help in any way, or a Deaf person who is enthusiastic, eager, and gives up time to labour for the Lord? The biggest difference may not be physical – attitude is very important.

# Hard of Hearing

This book is primarily concerned with people who are Deaf. As has been discussed, hard of hearing folk are a separate classification. But hard of hearing people make up the biggest category of those with a hearing loss, and physical changes to accommodate them can be made. For those who do not sign, but require assistance to hear, various Assistive Listening Devices (ALDs) are available. Here are some.

**Induction Audio Loop Systems.** 'Loop' systems are the most common of all the ALDs, because hearing aid users don't need any other special connecting device. These systems use a loop of insulated wire circling the worship area, which receives an electrical impulse from an amplifier. The public address system is plugged into this amplifier. In order to use the system, listeners must physically be within or near the loop area. A magnetic field is generated within the loop, which is picked up by the 'T' switch on the listener's hearing aid. The magnetic field is then re-converted through the hearing aid into sound. Fluorescent lighting can interfere with transmission and the signal can spill over into adjacent areas or rooms. It is possible for a loop user to be in the church kitchen making the after-service tea and be able to hear the sermon at the same time, so in a large church with several meetings happening concurrently in different halls, interference can occur.

**Infrared Systems.** IR systems use harmless invisible light beams in the infrared spectrum. IR light emitters can be connected to the existing church public address system. These emitters are located at various points in the worship area. The listener wears a receiver, rather like a stethoscope hanging under the chin. These can be plugged into the listener's hearing aids provided they have 'T' switches. Self-contained, portable amplifier/emitter units are available which can be wheeled from room to room.

An infrared device has impressive clarity regardless of where a person is sitting. But it will not work outdoors. It is also unable to penetrate solid walls. Line-of-sight placement of the emitters is best. Like light, however, the signal can bounce off walls and fill a room unless blocked by a solid barrier. IR is the only system that allows for confidential or private transmission in a closed room – ideal for counselling meetings.

**Frequency Modulation Systems.** FM systems also use the public address system. The PA is plugged into a transmitter, which broadcasts the signal to the worship area using an FM radio frequency. Listeners have a personal receiver and earphones to pick up the signal. The volume is adjusted to individual needs. As with the IR system, hearing aid users set their aids to the 'T' switch, and plug into the receiver.

FM systems have excellent sound quality and can be fully portable. That is, the transmitter can be taken to any room and plugged into a PA amplifier. All receivers are of course portable. Users can listen anywhere within a wide range indoors and out. The system transmits through walls, so nearby rooms should use different frequencies or channels. For this reason FM is inappropriate for private or confidential use. There may also be interference from other sources, such as passing taxicab radios or mobile phones.

## Job Done?

Having installed an ALD device, don't sit on your laurels. You should not install devices and just wait for users to come in. If your church has an ALD, then you should advertise it on

**'T'switch logo**

church posters, newsletters, etc. Display a sign in your entrance containing the hearing aid 'T' switch logo, and explain clearly and simply what users should do to pick up the signal. Do not install it and forget it – check it regularly. Use a testing device and ask the people who use the system if it is working and if the levels are comfortable. Check for 'dead areas', etc.

There are a good number of theatres and public venues that advertise these systems, but when hard of hearing people turn up they discover that they do not work, or work intermittently, because of poor or inadequate servicing. It is too late to remedy the problem quickly enough for that evening's event, so people are disappointed. It happens all too often.

## Changes Must be Made

We should seek to be aware of any needs, and not be afraid of changing things to make access and integration as comfortable as possible. Hearing people should change things for the comfort of Deaf people, surely not the other way round (which in many ways is impossible).

The 'equal rights activist' might say that Deaf people have had to make huge efforts to meet society's cultural and linguistic 'norms'. These efforts have been largely unnoticed, and despite them Deaf people are branded as failures. The Deaf community might well throw the blame on the hearing world, and charge it with consistently failing to provide services to meet Deaf needs.

However you view that statement, it may be a sad fact that your local Deaf people do not attend your church. They stay at home, or go to a different church which teaches doctrines not found in the Word of God. Why? Because your church has poor access, or integration is strained and uncomfortable. Think of it in this way: a hearing person is looking for a church, and stumbles upon one that uses a different language. The people in the church refuse to attempt communication, and no interpreter is available, or an interpreter is there, but is not up to the task. In such a situation, it does not matter what the doctrine is – it simply cannot be accessed.

The gospel can be offensive to some, but we dare not change the gospel; we must preach it in all its life-changing glory. But when the communication, or the church building itself, or the attitudes of the members, or their poor co-operation results in Deaf people feeling uncomfortable, this is something that can be changed. The most important change that can be made is to meet Deaf people's language needs. Churches can make that change, but it will take time and effort. Language is the first step. Lou Ann Walker (see bibliography) has commented: 'A deaf person raised Catholic will more likely attend a Baptist deaf service than a hearing mass.' Deaf people of many different backgrounds and persuasions will be drawn in if communication, access and an honest welcome are there.

## The 'Competition'

The Jehovah's Witnesses are running a sustained campaign to attract Deaf people. It is a distinct possibility that the next 'Witness' who comes to your door will be able to sign. They have interpreters and many good facilities, including glossy pictures, signed videos and DVDs for Deaf people. Their visitation of homes puts many churches to shame, and their efforts at attracting Deaf people does also. Some 'Witnesses' will take a Deaf person along with them *in case they meet* another Deaf person on the doorstep.

Have you visited a home where a Deaf person lives? Maybe you consider that the possibility is so low it is not worth making any special effort. Let us make the effort to please the Lord and reach Deaf people.

# SIX

# Learning British Sign Language

Where can I learn British Sign Language? How long does it take to become really fluent? What level of commitment is required? Are there exams I have to sit?

20,000 people and more every year learn sign language in British institutions. Most of those students are female. It is a popular subject, but the drop-out rate is high. For this reason course providers interview candidates, not for the purpose of assessing potential but commitment. If a prospective candidate cannot express more than a general interest, they may be disappointed. If you have a Deaf person in your family, you work with Deaf people or you want to include Deaf people in your church, a place is more likely to be offered.

Learning sign language certainly requires commitment, but many people fall in love with the language and the people who use it, and that sustains them as they learn. Part of the commitment may involve a career change, because after the first two levels of BSL the best learning route is usually via an NVQ, which is a vocational qualification and structured to support those who work with Deaf people.

The Council for the Advancement of Communication with Deaf People (CACDP) is the governing body for sign language qualifications, but that's not all. As of September 2007, their range of courses was as follows:

### Level 1 Certificates

Developing Awareness & Communication with Deaf & Deafblind People

British/Irish Sign Language ❶

### Level 2 Certificates

Communication with Deaf People

Communication with Deafblind People

Communication with Deafblind People (Manual)

British/Irish Sign Language ❷

The Living History of BSL

### Level 3 Certificates

Facilitating Communication with Deaf People (Lipspeaking skills)

Facilitating Communication with Deaf People (Manual Notetaking)

Facilitating Communication with Deaf People (Electronic Notetaking)

Communication with Deaf People

Facilitating Communication with Deaf People

Facilitating Communication with Deaf People (BSL)

Facilitating Communication with Deaf People (BSL and English)

Certificate for Lipspeakers, Manual Notetakers and Electronic Notetakers

Certificate for Speech to Text Reporters

Certificate for LSPs* with Deafblind People (Manual)

Modifying Written English Texts for Deaf People

Insights into Communication with Congenitally Deafblind People

British/Irish Sign Language (Non-NVQ Level 3 qualification) ❸

Level 3 NVQ in British/Irish Sign Language ❸

Language and Culture of Deaf People

### Level 4 NVQ

British/Irish Sign Language ❹

Interpreting (BSL/English) ❺

*Language Service Professionals.

54

This list is reproduced here to show the range on offer, to demonstrate that sign language is not the only choice, to reveal the attitude of CACDP, and the importance it gives to communication, access and understanding for Deaf and Deafblind people – they are not simply offering a language.

These courses are subject to amendment, so for up-to-date information enquire directly with CACDP. Their website (see appendix for details) has a list of colleges and schools that provide BSL courses. You may, however, enquire at your local adult education institution, because there are many BSL courses around the country. We have highlighted the natural route for learning BSL from the very beginning to becoming an interpreter, with the numbers ❶❷❸❹❺. Number ❸ has a choice of two: academic or vocational. This information is for clarity – do not ignore the other options. Many of the other courses are valuable and will help you identify other areas of support that may be required in your church.

The CACDP list of qualifications is not exhaustive. There are degree courses in Deaf Studies and postgraduate interpreting courses at some universities, and there are courses between levels. Some institutions will not teach, they will merely test and ratify an appropriate level of BSL skill, and help candidates submit an NVQ portfolio. More detail is not given here because information and opportunities change rapidly.

## What's it Like When You Start?

Candidates on the Level 1 Certificate in British/Irish Sign Language course will learn fingerspelling, vocabulary (food, animals, objects, places, etc.), Deaf greetings, etiquette and more. The learning curve for BSL is very steep at the start, and also, early in the course it will become obvious to candidates that a new way of thinking is required – a new view and perception must be taken on board – a perception of Deaf people and their culture and way of life. The intrinsic grammar of BSL is often inculcated rather than learned, and regular contact with Deaf people is important, and will speed the learning process.

At the start the teaching technique is firmly grounded in English words, word order and grammar, but as learning progresses, these features of English recede and BSL comes into its own, much like a plane taxiing along a runway – at some point the plane will take off, leaving the ground behind. As BSL students leave English behind and soar through the clouds, the 'air becomes thinner' – students need to collect evidence of their signing with others of similar or higher BSL skills, but the air is thinner because there are fewer people around of appropriate calibre. Students carry video cameras and tripods with them everywhere, because to attain the higher levels of BSL qualification there are film clips to collect – clips of themselves signing in various situations, such as discussion groups, informal and formal debates, and presentations. They have to cover productive criteria (signing) and receptive criteria (understanding someone else signing), and underpinning knowledge must be demonstrated. The thirst for vocabulary and grammar recedes and is replaced by an aim to produce beautiful signing. Clarity, expression and flow are admired as BSL students aim for fluency.

As a student progresses along the route to interpreter, more and more commitment is required. It is a sad fact that as individuals gain more and more skill and knowledge of BSL and interpreting, more barriers are thrown up to attaining qualification. There are few interpreters for many Deaf people, but the system is stacked against qualifying as an interpreter. It is hard work, and will cost dear. Do not be deterred but be warned: you must be prepared to work and strain for the prize.

It is vitally important to socialise and mix with Deaf people while you are learning, for three reasons:

1. You must demonstrate that you are interested in Deaf people, not just their language. If you interpret in church, but when the service finishes disappear to talk with your hearing friends, the Deaf people will be wary of you. They may think you are somehow using them.

2. You will learn the language more quickly if you mix with people who are using it, much the same as a trip to France will hone your French.

3. You will build up trust and empathy through social interaction, and the culture of Deafness will be more easily taken on board. This will aid your acquisition of the language.

It is theoretically possible to start from nothing and work through the levels to become an interpreter in five years. Practically speaking, however, that is virtually impossible. Course providers will recommend that you take a break between levels and forge more links with the Deaf community. This is partly because production of BSL is easier than reception. An individual can work hard and very quickly learn a large sign vocabulary and how to use it to produce signing with relative fluency. However, when a Deaf person signs back it is a different matter, because receiving signing with understanding takes much longer to learn. The worst thing is trying to understand fingerspelling – for 99% of hearing people this is a nightmare and even skilled and experienced interpreters have difficulties. Hearing people the world over struggle with this problem and many, mistakenly, think that the problem is only theirs.

In everyday conversation, a hearing person with a good level of BSL can understand the overall message from a Deaf person's signing, and if something is missed can fill in the gaps later using context, repetition and guesswork. Part of an interpreter's job, however, involves voicing over from a Deaf person's signing without the luxury of time and silence. That is the hardest part of an interpreter's work, having to voice the information with accuracy when it is produced. It is an incredible skill that takes time, practice, confidence and integration with the Deaf community.

Do not be deterred or afraid – many people have trodden the path before you and succeeded.

## SEVEN

# Interpreting

What is the role of a BSL interpreter? How can I find someone to interpret in my church? Are there any other people that can aid communication? If I learn sign language, do I have to be qualified to interpret?

## Who is an Interpreter?

A BSL interpreter listens to speech and converts it into another language, in this instance, British Sign Language (there are other methods of communication which will be discussed later). The interpreter also converts BSL into speech. It is a two-way interaction. Also there is cultural mediation.

There is a national shortage of qualified BSL interpreters. In September 2006, there were only 298 registered qualified interpreters serving England, Wales and Northern Ireland (around 80 per cent of them were women). These are interpreters on the lists of the Council for the Advancement of Communication with Deaf People (CACDP). In 2002 the Royal National Institute for Deaf People put the ratio at one for every 400 Deaf people. In the same year the British Deaf Association quoted one for every

**There is a national shortage of qualified BSL interpreters.**

thousand Deaf people. Precise information is impossible to obtain. To compound that, only a small percentage are willing to take on religious work. That is because most interpreters do not know many specialised theological signs or feel comfortable in a church environment. Also, most importantly, the interpreter needs to have an understanding of the nature of the material being interpreted.

## The Interpreter's Understanding of Theology

Let us suppose a fictitious interpreter is asked to work in a medical situation, but is unaware of the particular medical procedure that a doctor is describing. The interpreter thinks everything is OK, but there is a risk that a faulty meaning is interpreted. The Deaf patient may misunderstand what the doctor is suggesting, which could lead to disaster. By the same token, an interpreter working in a courtroom must be aware, not only of legal matters, but also of court etiquette and procedure. Interpreters working in church would struggle if they were unaware of theology, hymnody and Bible language.

Prospective interpreters not accustomed to attending church will probably decline the assignment. Indeed, interpreters have a code of ethics which states that they should not take on an assignment that is beyond their ability. Also, interpreters who regularly work in church situations will often have their own church, and may need to interpret for the Deaf people there, or may be involved in other areas and have their own responsibilities. Also, interpreters want to have weekends off like other people.

Don't be discouraged. You may be able to find someone willing to help. When you do so, you may discover that a charge is levied. This is entirely acceptable. Some interpreters work on a freelance basis. They are professionals with a high level of training and experience. They are entirely right to expect payment at nationally agreed rates. However, some may leave it to the church to pay only expenses, or will accept a gift. Whatever the arrangement, be sure to settle the issue before the assignment, so everyone knows where they stand.

## Working with Interpreters in Church

There are many considerations. The work starts well before the church service does. If you are the one to liaise with the interpreter, you will need to make a nuisance of yourself. The ideal is to give the interpreter full sermon notes, readings, hymns and announcements one full week before the interpreting assignment. The interpreter will ask for these, because the interpreter will be the only link between the church service and the Deaf people. Any prior warning of subject matter, hymns, Scripture texts, etc., will help preparation and aid transfer of the true meaning of the worship. An interpreter will want to have the Bible readings with enough time to sit down and study them, possibly with other versions of the Bible, to get the meaning as simple and clear as possible.

That is the ideal, but we live in the real world. You can hassle and persuade, but it may be you can only provide the hymns, the readings, and the Scripture text on which the sermon is based the night before. If that is all you can do, then make sure you do it. Get the information to the interpreter as soon as you can.

Give your regular interpreter a copy of the hymn book you use, so in future you only need to provide numbers and do not have to photocopy the full hymn and fax it.

Sermons that involve jumping about from verse to verse are a nightmare to interpret. The interpreter needs to find each reading, interpret it and be ready for the next very quickly. When the sermon involves multiple references it is essential the interpreter knows what they are beforehand, so the Bible can be flagged up with markers and the interpreter can go straight to each quickly.

## The Day of Rest

Interpreting a church service is hard work. Actually this is a gross understatement – it is true to say that interpreting a church service is a physically draining exercise, and involves contorted mental gymnastics. When the interpreter has finished she (80% of interpreters are women) may not be able to speak coherently. It is one of the most mentally and physically demanding jobs. There are safeguards, however, which include co-working. In a secular assignment an interpreter will work for around 20 minutes, then the co-worker will take over. This maintains freshness of concentration, and also means that the working interpreter can be backed up by the resting one if a thought is lost or a meaning can be made clearer.

Realistically you will probably only have one interpreter. All the worship needs to be interpreted: hymns, prayers, readings, announcements, sermon. Even after the service the work is not finished, because some hearing folk may take the opportunity to chat with the Deaf folk, and so the conversation must be interpreted to and fro. The interpreter has been working for two hours, usually alone. Concentrating in such an unrelenting way for so long saps energy. Someone has to be aware that physical needs must be met. Look after your interpreter, and try to make her visit with you as comfortable and enjoyable as possible, or she may not want to return for a regular assignment.

## The First Time an Interpreter Comes

Ideally you will need to meet the interpreter at your church before the date of the assignment to discuss and decide on a number of things. Where to stand – on the platform or in another area of the church? (Some interpreters may ask if it is acceptable to interrupt the speaker to clarify a point.) You must provide a music stand for the interpreter to put a hymn book and Bible on, to lead the singing, and sign the readings.

Do you have a pre-service prayer meeting? The interpreter may want to attend that, or even be present with the pastor just prior to the service, and walk in together onto the platform. The interpreter will need a seat, facing the congregation, and a glass of water. (This is very important – when interpreting the mouth becomes very dry and the lips need constant moistening. It is a fact of life – ask any interpreter.) Adequate lighting is important. A gloomy corner is not the best place for signing hands to be seen, and the light must be on the interpreter, not behind. Also the order of service must be discussed so there are no surprises.

It may be that a specific area of the church is best for your Deaf people, such as a gallery or anteroom, so the interpreter and the Deaf people can make it theirs. The reason could be that your church is small, or is usually very full, or the service is filmed, and an interpreter will present problems of camera location. This, however, may be a bone of contention. The interpreter will want to be as prominent as possible, not to be seen and admired, but to ensure that Deaf people are given as much access and opportunity as hearing people. When there is a difference of opinion, one way of resolving it is to present the problem to the Deaf people themselves and ask what they think is best.

## Are All Interpreters the Same?

There are different interpreting techniques. One is to interpret very nearly word for word. This technique is called Sign Supported English (SSE). Other interpreters will use BSL.

Using BSL means that a longer 'lag-time' is used during which the meaning of a phrase is digested and then signed in the grammar of BSL. The translation will not then be exactly as spoken in the source language, but the meaning will be given in the target language.

©Pascal Johnson

Then there is a technique called lipspeaking, where the interpreter will usually sit near the Deaf receiver and silently mouth the words clearly. Where words are similar to another word, fingerspelling of the problem letter makes it clear. Lipspeaking follows the spoken words exactly. There are training courses for lipspeaking (again, there is a national shortage of lipspeakers). Ask your Deaf people what they prefer, don't just presume that all interpreters are the same and book without thought.

Having said that, most Deaf people who use BSL as their first language will prefer a BSL interpreter. This is because they think in BSL, so there is a problem when an SSE interpreter comes along. Deaf people are forced to do some interpreting for themselves, from English into BSL. Ten minutes or so of that and the concentration begins to suffer.

Most Deaf people who have lost their hearing later in life and have a good grasp of written English will be fine with SSE, and good lipreaders will be happy with lipspeaking.

At a conference where many Deaf people are expected, a good organiser will lay on interpreters who work in BSL and SSE, a lipspeaker, a speech-to-text reporter, Deafblind interpreters and notetakers, all in different parts of the auditorium. Assistive Listening Devices will be in place for hearing aid users (see illustration opposite).

Don't be confused or bewildered. All this information is simply to make you aware of the scope of the subject, and what is available. Again, the advice is – ask your Deaf people what they prefer, and come to a mutually agreed solution. Assume nothing.

On the subject of Assistive Listening Devices, an induction loop is a basic and inexpensive facility to provide in a church, as discussed before in chapter 5. If your church borrows a building for worship – a local school for instance – there are portable loop systems available.

## The Interpreting Code

So you've found an interpreter after much searching. Now what about doctrine? What denomination or persuasion is the interpreter? Yours is a Baptist church, the interpreter is an Anglican. Does it matter? Will the sign used to interpret 'baptism' represent the Anglican or Baptistic method? Here are a few considerations.

Whatever method is used – BSL, SSE, lipspeaking, etc., – the interpreter is duty-bound to interpret what is heard.

Interpreters may be required to communicate views that are not theirs. This is an occupational hazard. If those views are particularly uncomfortable, then the only acceptable option for the interpreter is to decline future assignments. There must be a period during which the church and the interpreter get to know each other.

The interpreter should know the Baptistic sign for 'baptism'. If the sermon is debating the difference between Anglican and Baptistic methods, then the interpreter will use the signs for both. We must give the interpreter the benefit of the doubt. If the Deaf worshippers are unsure of a word or concept, then they will ask later, and a subsequent transcript, if available, will clear everything up.

The interpreter will be worshipping as well. It is the Holy Spirit's work to give light and understanding. We all have views that need to be moulded by God's Word. Do not hesitate to invite an interpreter from another denomination if there are none available from yours.

## The Gender Issue

A Deaf couple planned their wedding. She was hard of hearing, a very good lipreader and could speak well. Her husband-to-be needed a BSL interpreter. The only interpreter who could be found was a woman. At the wedding he was asked to pronounce his vows, which he did in sign language. The lady interpreter duly interpreted this into speech. It meant that guests heard both sets of vows spoken by women.

There are more fundamental issues, and some cases require definite decisions. An interpreter was booked by a church deacon. She later phoned to inform him frankly that she was a homosexual. She knew the stance of the church, and felt that she had to give him the opportunity to think again about the booking. Because she actively promoted her chosen orientation, it may have given people the wrong signals of the church's standpoint. She was thanked for her honesty, the booking was declined, but the deacon said that she was most welcome to attend the services.

Some churches insist that the interpreter must be a man. As the interpretation is an extension of the preaching, they say, the gender should follow the New Testament pattern. This is something you need to think seriously about. The role of the interpreter has been equated with a telephone – someone who simply transmits data from one place to another and has no personal input. Although this is true in some ways, the reality is different (research papers about this subject abound). That aside, there are far more female interpreters than males. In fact, there are pitifully few male students learning BSL at every level, so it could be that you are closing yourself off from any work amongst Deaf people, because you cannot find a male interpreter. Clearly there must be flexibility, but no confusion. The pastor and church leaders must be clear about what they are overseeing.

## The Invisible Interpreter

It is the interpreter's aim to be as invisible as possible – to be the 'vehicle.' If the preacher refers to the interpreter in the service, or publicly asks if delivery speed needs to be slower, then 'anonymity' is broken, and it may lead to embarrassment. If reference must be made, limit it to an introductory welcome, much the same as welcoming a visiting preacher, then leave the interpreter to do the job, and provide the support to make that happen.

## Interpreting or Communicating?

In Britain today there is an army of communication support workers (CSWs). These folk are not qualified interpreters, but in practice work as such. They work mainly in education, supporting Deaf students of all ages. Some are climbing the qualification ladder toward interpreter level, but many regard their job as their vocation. Their work is varied: they not only interpret for Deaf students in education, they take notes, modify textbooks and teaching resources, teach Deaf-awareness to hearing tutors, support students with life skills and so on. There are professional qualifications for CSWs, and a national association that supports them. CSWs exist because there is such a shortage of qualified interpreters, and many interpreters prefer not to work in education. CSWs do not usually work in healthcare, and should not work in the legal system or for the police, although sometimes they are pressured to do so.

CSWs may not have interpreting qualifications, but in some ways may be more experienced and have a broader role than simply interpreting, although this is their primary function. Whatever is the case, if you engage the services of a CSW for interpreting in church, she will be careful to make clear, both to you and the Deaf people, what her levels of qualification, expertise and experience are.

There are interpreters and CSWs who are Deaf themselves, and some are hard of hearing, relying on 'loop' systems, etc. We know a professional CSW who is profoundly Deaf. She relies on expert lipreading and is very good at her job. There are some international interpreters who are Deaf, and interpret from one sign language to another.

# Are You Willing?

Now here is something for you to think seriously about. If you find an interpreter (or CSW), she may not be able to meet all your requirements. If you book an interpreter through an agency then you may find the cost becomes a heavy burden, especially as more and more meetings require interpreting. If a need is there, and it is impossible to find or afford a professional, then someone must step in.

This is a bone of contention. It is wrong to learn a few basic signs and pass yourself off as an interpreter. Interpreting is a skilled profession, concerned about clarity of interpretation and competence. Horror stories abound.

On a personal note, when I had been learning sign language for only a year, I helped a Deaf friend when he moved home. I went with him into the local council's offices and interpreted. Later when I told some other Deaf friends what I'd done they were horrified. They explained the potential problems. Was I working for the council or for my friend? What would happen if there was a legal problem later on, and the council blamed me because I had given the wrong meaning? I was not insured, and some may say I was dabbling in areas I was not qualified for. I explained that I had told the council's representative that I was a friend and was asked by him to help. In that capacity I was acting as a sort of communicator. Everything was double-checked, and the paperwork was shown to my friend for verification. He and I were happy that the true meaning was understood, and the council's representative thanked me for helping. However, the reaction of my other Deaf friends served to make me more careful and wary of situations I may not be adequate for. Having said that, any hearing person who has Deaf friends will find themself naturally being asked to do various interpreting tasks. The hardest thing then is to say no.

## Should I Get 'Stuck In'?

Some churches have access for Deaf people, but have signers with very basic skills, doing what they can. Some churches know there is a need, but don't know where to start. This is a plea to think hard about providing access, but not to run before you can walk. Be aware of the pitfalls, use professional interpreters when you can, but do not neglect your duty. Roll up your sleeves and get stuck in. Start by supporting a visiting interpreter in church services by signing hymns and prayers and Bible readings. Aim at becoming a qualified interpreter yourself.

## The Code of Ethics

The interpreter's code of ethics is summarised thus: behave responsibly and professionally, never stop learning, safeguard standards, offer other interpreters help and respect other professions. Interpret as best you can without adding or subtracting, and do not accept work beyond your competence. Treat information and other assignments confidentially, do not take sides or use any interpreted information to benefit yourself. Do not offer advice or opinions in an assignment and do not cancel an assignment (or delegate) without good reason. If you must cancel, try to find a suitably qualified substitute. The code of ethics is all good common sense.

Theory is all very well, but in practice, interpreters are faced with difficult ethical choices constantly. There is the case of an interpreter who supports a Deaf man who has an appointment at the benefit office. The very next day the interpreter is assigned to the same man at the housing office, where he proceeds to give the housing officer different personal information – he is lying to gain advantage. What should the interpreter do? Again, picture the scene in a hospital where an interpreter has been asked to work with a Deaf expectant mum who is having a pre-birth scan. The mum-to-be has told the nurse through the interpreter that she doesn't want to know the sex of the baby. The nurse forgets this and lets the information slip. Now we have a problem. The interpreter's code of ethics must be honoured. The interpreter must let the Deaf 'client' know everything that is said. That is what interpreters do. After all, if the client could hear, then she would instantly know the information. What would you do? If it was your friend and you were interpreting for her, then the answer may be easier – you would probably keep the information to yourself. What about professional ethics, however? Maybe you would tell the mum-to-be that the nurse has let it slip, but give no details. This may not be the best action because the client may know that it is easier to identify a male baby. These are typical of the ethical choices that interpreters have to make in their working day.

In a secular assignment the Deaf 'client' has a right to know that the interpreter is a member of the professional body, bound by the code of ethics, with a proper level of training and experience, and covered by professional indemnity insurance. Interpreters are sometimes required to wear badges showing their level of competence, especially on a first assignment.

## A Higher Code

If you are interpreting in your own church it is a little different. There will not be any legal proceedings for giving wrong meanings. There is no misunderstanding who the employer is, and you are working voluntarily. If you are interpreting for the Deaf people in your church (and not visitors who may come in) then you are doing your friends a service, and they will forgive you for any gaffs. However, there is a higher authority. You must understand that you are bound by Scripture, together with the preacher, to rightly divide the word of truth *(2 Timothy 2:15)*. This is far more serious and binding than any earthly code of ethics. Obedience to that higher authority must be your overriding goal. Ironically, qualified interpreters will tell you that religious assignments are far more difficult than secular work. In fact, we have heard of some Christian interpreters who will not work in church at all, so the challenge is there.

Who will take up the gauntlet? At the back of this book you will find some useful contacts for finding BSL courses around the country, and also the best places to buy signing books, videos and other resources. Find other like-minded people in your church willing to learn BSL, and proceed with the objective of firstly communicating with your Deaf friends, and then providing interpreters from within the fellowship.

Although the task may seem daunting, when you enroll on a BSL course the time will speed along and you will soon discover you can converse, and, amazingly, Deaf people will understand you! Your confidence will rise. Watch other interpreters when you can. Seek out the company of Deaf people. Communication will blossom.

## Who Can Check Whether I am Doing OK?

It is an excellent idea to ask a qualified interpreter to assess your signing skills, and give you advice. You will then know the blunt truth or receive an encouraging word. Do not ask the Deaf people to assess you – they can only advise on clarity of signing, not whether you are interpreting accurately. They can access only half of the information. Also Deaf people may give a positive response just to encourage you. Some may say they understand when they do not, because they feel you are testing them, and they don't want to admit they don't understand.

Any attempt to interpret must obviously be done with the blessing and support of the church leaders. Having obtained that, sit next to your Deaf friends in church, or turn your chair around and face them. Start by interpreting the announcements, then the prayer. Hymns are a great learning ground – watching Deaf people singing is very instructive.

Who knows? With the help of your Deaf friends quite a little team of you may become proficient. If you feel confident to attempt the sermon, don't begin by standing at the front of the congregation. When you are learning you will need to clarify signs and thoughts as the message proceeds, so there will need to be interaction, which may distract other worshippers. Your Deaf people will ask you to clarify signs both during a sermon and afterwards, and also give you advice. When you start you will probably be interpreting in a sort of SSE (Sign Supported English), which is difficult for some Deaf people to follow for long periods. That will change as you progress.

## But How Dare I Presume to be an Interpreter?

Qualified interpreters will not blame you for poaching their work. They only have the interests of Deaf people at heart. Qualified interpreters, however, are always concerned that accuracy of meaning is compromised by those who are not qualified to interpret. This is a constant problem, especially for church situations. Deaf people want to attend your church, but you cannot find any appropriately skilled interpreters. You have a duty to provide some means of imparting understanding, using one or more of the methods discussed, best suited to your skills and the Deaf people's needs.

If you and the Deaf people in your church feel that interpreting is the best route, it is important for a group of you to attempt the task. Each can check and suggest and encourage the others. A 40-minute sermon, for instance, is very taxing on the concentration. After 20 minutes or so, the interpretation will become less sharp and tiredness will effect the signing. With a team of people it will become easier.

If you want to interpret in church, do not stop with an adequate grasp of BSL – aim at going the whole way. Good Christian interpreters are few and far between, so aim at becoming one. Who knows, there may be a conference or seminary that is in need of someone like you? At the moment there are very few Deaf Christians in Bible colleges and seminaries because of the shortage of Christian interpreters.

The key to learning BSL quickly is interaction with Deaf people. This cannot be stressed enough. They will help you, correct you, encourage and tease you. Many people on BSL courses don't know any Deaf people. Because of this the BSL tutor will make arrangements for the class to meet in a local Deaf club, where Deaf people congregate. These are in churches, pubs, clubs, etc., some where alcohol is sold, so it might be a problem for you. You will have a distinct advantage if Deaf people attend your church.

When you are learning, the appearance of a real live interpreter is a great treat. Sit with your Deaf friends and feast your eyes on the eloquence, speed and clarity of the interaction. Do not be discouraged, but learn as much as you can. Watching interpreters work is an enlightening experience.

## Some Hints

As a basic rule, only BSL NVQ Level 3 signers and above should be interpreting in church. If you are not at this level (or even if you are) here is a summary of some of the practical points we have been discussing:

1. Get as much prior information as you can, so you are well prepared (that means you are presenting material rather than interpreting). Photocopy the information and give it to the Deaf people when the service finishes.

2. Ask someone more experienced to watch you and give 'feedback'. Find opportunities to work with other interpreters.

3. Remember that Deaf people do not know if the interpreter is good, because they don't know how much information is missing. Deaf people may be happy with your signing, but they do not know how good your interpreting skills are.

4. Have a serious aim to develop your skills. Do not rest on your laurels, content with what you have done. Aim at interpreter status.

5. Ask a hearing worshipper to take notes, with the brief to use simple English words and phrases, then photocopy them and distribute them as hand-outs.

## Training Up the Younger Generation

One final comment in this chapter – think about the children in your church. Often the best interpreters are those who are native signers. These are hearing people who have Deaf parents and have grown up through childhood interpreting in the family. They are skilled signers partly because they have started early. Children are fascinated by sign language. It is a great pity that sign language courses are generally only available to those aged 16 and over, unless the local school has a teacher who offers BSL as an after-school enrichment activity. This is changing – we hear news of schools starting to include BSL in their curriculum. If young people in your church show an interest, encourage them. If you know BSL, then teach them what you know. Buy signing books as birthday presents. Display the fingerspelling alphabet in the Sunday School room. Encourage them to communicate with the church Deaf people. By doing this you are laying up workers for the future. You may also be providing another career option in a field where there is a great need.

EIGHT

# What Theology is Right for Deaf People?
Current Trends Discussed

**D**oes the Bible have anything to say for Deaf people today? **Is the Bible a book only for hearing people, or can Deaf people find what they need there also? Are there any guidelines in the Scripture for how the church can approach the inclusion of Deaf people?**

The answer to those questions is a resounding 'yes', but before we can explore those questions, we must look at some current modern theologies that are proposed. These are being promoted with the aim of providing Deaf people with access to the Bible, to church life and to worship. Unfortunately, the aim of such theologies is not to revere and follow what the Bible has to say, but rather, what amounts to misappropriation of the Bible to fit in with prevailing criteria, rights and culture. These modern theologies are discussed here so that people can be aware of them, and not be misled by their seeming reasonableness and helpfulness for the Deaf case.

## Deaf 'Liberation Theology'

This is a theology that aims to 'liberate' people – in fact, to liberate entire oppressed groups. At first sight it seems to be a flexible and creative theology. It reasons as follows – if strict traditional theology is advocated for everyone, then inevitably some people will be oppressed. It focuses on 'contexts' – producing different theologies for different groups. 'We need to look at the Bible from a Deaf perspective,' it says. 'It's not good enough to be given hearing worship through interpreters. Deaf people should have it their way. After all, the Lord Jesus did not want anyone to be oppressed, and Paul says we are all equal.' In fact, the apostle Paul is cited as the first 'Liberation Theologian', because of the so-called rift between him and the other apostles about Jewish culture and the new Christian church. Paul was the champion of the Gentiles. The reasoning is that Paul recognised that different groups needed their own theology. Deaf people are such a group, so they have to be militant, and form their own theology. Liberation theology says that the Bible has not changed, but it was written by hearing people for hearing people; so Deaf people must look at the Bible afresh, within the context of their culture and history. Deaf people should do it for themselves. The Bible must fit with their culture.

This is a militant view that takes no prisoners. Deaf people and their rights have become more important than the truth of God, once and for all revealed. Liberation theology has employed mistaken contemporary interpretation methods. The Bible has become open to any interpretation by anyone, and Deaf people have a right to join the free-for-all.

## 'Struggle Theology'

This view has at its heart the so-called 'struggle' of the apostle Paul, referred to above. Its published aim is to throw down a challenge to the Nonconformist, conservative sector of the British church, because it has consistently failed Deaf people. Although its aim may be well-intentioned, its theology is flawed. Its underpinning tenet is that God supposedly gave

Paul the task of including Gentiles in the established Jewish church. The Gentiles were despised by the Jews, so it was an uphill struggle. Paul's whole life from then on was supposedly full of struggle, controversy and pain as he tried to achieve this.

The tension between the proud Jews with their strong culture, and the Gentiles who tried to access the Jewish religion without accepting the ceremonial baggage, is equated with the tension between the dominant hearing church and the Deaf person. Paul is perceived to be the hero again – the champion for people outside the Jewish fold – a good example for the Deaf case.

Such a theology is misguided, because if a worthy challenge is to be aimed at conservative churches that respect the inerrant Word of God, it must come from a theology that is reasoned clearly from the Bible, not a 'read between the lines' approach. This is most definitely of that sort – building theories out of mistakenly perceived issues.

We must be clear about this – Paul's God-given career was not political nor cultural. He was not working to include Gentiles in the old Jewish order. It was very simple, and we can read it from his own pen: 'For Christ sent me...to preach the gospel' *(1 Corinthians 1:17)*. The fact is that God had now brought in His spiritual church – the church of Jesus Christ. Paul's mission was to preach the gospel, so that people would be saved, and then become members of the new spiritual church of Jesus Christ.

The struggles Paul had were against culturally militant Jews who followed him around to disrupt his work and do away with him. They were agents of the devil, and they hated the name of Jesus Christ. It was Christ Himself Who gave Paul his ministry. Paul's mission was to preach to the Gentiles, Peter's was to preach to the Jews. What were they to preach? The very same gospel of Jesus Christ. The new spiritual church was being formed and built up. Jews and Gentiles had equal status in the eyes of God. Jewish birth and culture could not help. 'For all have sinned, and come short of the glory of God' *(Romans 3:23)*.

Struggle theology cites the clash between Peter and Paul as an example of Paul trying to include Gentiles in the Jewish church against the wishes of the other apostles. It is true that Paul and Peter clashed. Paul challenged Peter because he had slipped and compromised and had become afraid of offending the strongly cultural Jews. That clash is recorded by Paul himself in *Galatians 2*. Paul was clarifying that Christ's new church was spiritual and not based on any particular culture. To illustrate his point, Paul reminded the Galatians that he had correctly rebuked Peter to demonstrate that Christian Jews should not be afraid to let go of their Jewish culture. Indeed, they should follow Christ alone.

We dare not use Paul's struggles as a model for including Deaf people in the church. His was the struggle between the devil and the Lord – the flesh and the Spirit – the old and the new. The established, but unbiblical, Jewish culture of 'works' hindered him as he laboured for the new spiritual church of Jesus Christ.

The irony is that Paul's theology agreed 100% with the Old Testament – the scrolls that many Jewish leaders fanatically treasured, but consistently failed to correctly understand. Whenever Paul preached to Jews, he used the Old Testament to prove that Jesus Christ was the Messiah. Paul did not deviate from the Scriptures. Indeed, God used him as an inspired writer to add to the Scriptures. All Paul's writings confirmed and agreed with the Old Testament; and when the canon of Scripture was complete, Paul's contribution dovetailed into the Word of Truth, given to us by God Himself. Paul did not develop his own theology to include a marginalised group. If we want a model for the inclusion of Deaf people we must look elsewhere.

## Deaf Eschatology

Another new theology has been proposed. As it is well nigh impossible to integrate Deaf people into hearing churches with real parity, this might help – think of Heaven. Everything will be sorted out in Heaven. Wrongs will all be righted. But let's bring that forward and view Deaf people in an eternal perspective. We should live in the expectation of the return of the Lord Jesus. On that day everything will then be made right and set in order. This new theology says that Christ's death and resurrection were less about redemption and more a demonstration of His power over our fears and suffering, especially those of groups like Deaf people. It advises us to look forward to when Christ comes again, because, it is reasoned, redemption will only truly happen then.

This theology views the Trinity in a new way: the Trinity, or the 'equality of God', teaches us that we are all equal, and therefore one person should not have power over another – this seems to fit well with the Deaf/hearing struggle.

This is more a socialist theory than a Biblical theology, and lacks any clear practical structure for church life. It is a thinly-veiled challenge to perceived institutionalism in the church, and denies the Holy Spirit's work in the heart.

## A Flawed View of Scripture

These and other contemporary views spring from a mistaken interpretation of the Bible. The Bible has its own rules for interpretation, and all true Christians have a duty to find out what they are. An increasing problem is that many Christians have taken on board the ideas of Bible critics who are not true believers. The Bible has become just like any other book. It is fashionable today to review and attack and glean whatever theory is required.

The Bible should be given its rightful status as the inspired Word of God. We should approach it with reverence, eager to learn. We should not try to fit the Bible into our own criteria, rights and culture. It is no ordinary book. The Bible was not written by hearing people for hearing people. Such a statement is not helpful, and clearly reveals the mistaken mindset of the person making it. The Bible was written by God Himself. Through the Holy Spirit, God inspired His chosen writers with His very words. He used the writer's own style, but every word was inspired. It is God's Word indeed, and any other view denies Biblical inspiration.

The Bible was written for all people – in every culture and situation, and with every level of understanding. It is true that many Deaf people find written language hard to access, but this is something that can be positively addressed. The point is that the truths of the Bible are accessible to all, because the Holy Spirit helps us to understand them. When the Holy Spirit is absent, we miss the true meaning, whether we are Deaf or hearing. A humanistic reading of the text will always miss the spiritual point. *1 Corinthians 2:14* explains that the truth of God is spiritually understood: 'But the natural man receiveth not the things of the Spirit of God: for they are foolishness unto him: neither can he know them, because they are spiritually discerned.' This is where many people make a grave mistake.

For a more comprehensive and lucid treatment of this subject, see *Not Like Any Other Book,* by Dr Peter Masters (details in the bibliography).

## True Deaf Theology

There is much comfort and blessing for the Deaf person in the Bible. It meets identity, communication and relationship needs, because it meets the needs of the soul. We do not need to panic and search for a new Deaf theology to emulate the world's increasing social and political inclusion for Deaf people. We have something better – the Word of God, unchanged for thousands of years, relevant for all ages and states and conditions of people. We dare not change the Bible, or search for a 'new' Deaf theology, supposedly undiscovered for hundreds of years. We need not, because the Bible is sufficient. But how can we discover these things? Show us the verses for Deaf people!

We must not start with diversity, but with unity. *Galatians 3:28* says, 'There is neither Jew nor Greek, there is neither bond nor free, there is neither male nor female: for ye are all one in Christ Jesus.' We can include many different groups in the verse, such as Deaf and hearing, because diversity is not the important thing, it is the point of unity that is important: '...all one in Christ Jesus'. We start with Him – Jesus Christ can heal the soul. Other criteria like politics, background, upbringing, gender, culture, language, etc., were of little importance to the Lord.

## Marginalised Groups

The Lord Jesus positively reached out to people from marginalised groups and blessed them. He did it far too many times for it to be a coincidence. Here are a few examples.

**1. John 4.** The sexually impure woman by the well. A Samaritan, despised by the Jews. That was of no consequence to the Lord Jesus, and He offered her 'living water'.

**2. John 5.** The disabled man by the pool of Bethesda. No one would help him, but the Lord Jesus gave him help, and more.

**3. Matthew 20.** The two blind men who called out to the Lord Jesus. The people discriminated against them and told them to be quiet. They called out the more, and the Lord Jesus did not ignore them.

**4. Mark 5.** The man possessed by evil spirits. He was a social outcast. People had tried to chain him, and he lived in the tombs. The Lord Jesus freed him and brought him back into society.

**5. Mark 10.** That neglected and marginalised section of society – children. The Lord Jesus reproved the disciples when they tried to keep the children away. His view was that children are vitally important. He used them as an example, and explained that we must all become like 'little children', or we cannot enter the kingdom of God.

**6. Mark 7.** Finally (*our* final one, although there are many more) a Deaf man. Incidentally, Jewish Deaf people experienced quite a degree of legal discrimination. The ancient Jewish *Talmud*, a huge collection of laws and traditions, did not allow Deaf people to take part in any civil or legal events because these had an *oral* precedent. Deaf people were not able to access education. They were not allowed to own homes or land, although sometimes the community donated a small plot. If they owned anything of value it could be taken away from them. In many ways they were marginalised. The Lord had a different agenda. He gave the man hearing and also clear speech, thus giving him access to those things that were denied before. (See note 1 at end of chapter.)

# A Cultural Challenge

The Lord Jesus drew people together spiritually, but He rejected those who came with their own culture and viewpoints. When people came to Christ, He changed them. He gave them spiritual life, but the people had to change. They had to change their thinking, their culture, their attitudes, their way of life. There are many examples. Here are two.

**The disciples** – some were fishermen. They had their own fishing business, which had probably been in the family for generations. The Lord called them, and they left everything to follow Him. Peter himself said in *Matthew 19:27,* 'Behold, we have forsaken all, and followed thee.'

**Zacchaeus** – he was rich, but he had cheated many people. The Lord saved him, and he repaid what he had stolen many times over. The rich cheat changed and became honest and generous. A contrasting event is described in *Mark 10:21–22.* The Lord told another rich man his life had to change. He had to sell everything and give it all away to the poor. He could not, so the blessing was not given.

The Lord Jesus said in *Mark 8:34,* 'Whosoever will come after me, let him deny himself, and take up his cross, and follow me.' Again, in *Luke 14:33,* 'Whosoever he be of you that forsaketh not all that he hath, he cannot be my disciple.'

Many Jews, especially the leaders of the Jews, could not change, because their attachment to their culture was too strong. Their culture had developed over the years, and departed from the clear truths of the Old Testament. They failed to identify that the prophecies, the psalms, and the details of the Jewish ceremonial law, were all pointing to Jesus Christ. The Lord reasoned with them and warned them, to help them understand that they must let their culture go and seek forgiveness from God, but they grew the more angry. Christ said in *Matthew 23:23,* 'Woe unto you, scribes and Pharisees, hypocrites! for ye pay tithe of mint and anise and cummin, and have omitted the weightier matters of the law, judgment, mercy, and faith: these ought ye to have done, and not to leave the other undone.'

The apostle Paul recognised the same truth. He realised that he needed to change. What did he say about his proud Jewish culture? *Philippians 3:5-8,* 'Circumcised the eighth day, of the

85

stock of Israel, of the tribe of Benjamin, an Hebrew of the Hebrews; as touching the law, a Pharisee; concerning zeal, persecuting the church; touching the righteousness which is in the law, blameless. But what things were gain to me, those I counted loss for Christ. Yea doubtless, and I count all things but loss for the excellency of the knowledge of Christ Jesus my Lord: for whom I have suffered the loss of all things, and do count them but dung, that I may win Christ.'

Willingness to change is part of coming to the Lord and being saved. If a person says he or she is a Christian, but remains unchanged, that person has missed the point of seeking and finding the Lord. A big change happens, and it is called repentance. No repentance – no spiritual life.

It is also true that genuine Christian people must change as they travel on their spiritual journey. We read our Bibles – we are challenged, because the Holy Spirit helps us to understand deeper things. We examine ourselves, and we know we have to change. We should not look at the Bible and think, 'OK, what can I change there to fit the Deaf case better?' No, we would be tampering with the very words of God. It is not the Bible that has to change, it is us.

What can we learn from these things? There is a challenge here for both hearing and Deaf people.

**Hearing people.** Be prepared to change. The Lord Jesus blessed representatives from many groups of marginalised people, thereby including them. Be careful to follow His example and do not treat Deaf people with indifference. Deaf Christians should be offered the same status in the church as hearing Christians, and their needs as people should be addressed, not in a patronising way, but with respect and understanding. Consider *Exodus 4:11,* 'And the LORD said unto him, Who hath made man's mouth? or who maketh the dumb, or deaf, or the seeing, or the blind? have not I the LORD?' God made Deaf people. They are not a mistake; He made them Deaf in His great and glorious plan. That verse alone should change our perception and bring Deaf and hearing closer in the church. (See note 2 at end of chapter.)

**Deaf people.** Be prepared to change. Do not stand up for your rights. Enter into a dialogue for change, and respect every small change that takes place. Be patient. Do not insist that Deaf culture is brought into the church. Remember that there are some damaging aspects of that culture, such as gossip and backstabbing which are rife. Christ's culture is about mutual love and forgiving one another, and esteeming people more highly than yourself.

True believers, Deaf and hearing, should strive to be more like Christ every day. The Lord Jesus was always giving. He gave Himself to the point of death, and beyond. As we seek to be more like Him, we will be drawn closer to each other.

Some Deaf people will not be happy with this reasoning. The world and its struggle for human rights has handed power to the Deaf lobby. Self-assertiveness is king. Hearing people have abused Deaf people for too long, and now it is time for payback.

But what did Paul say? 'Submitting yourselves one to another in the fear of God' *(Ephesians 5:21).* That is the key to access for Deaf people. This sentiment is well articulated in this verse from the pen of *Charles Wesley* (1707-88).

> *Sweetly may we all agree,*
> *Touched with truest sympathy;*
> *Prove there's neither bond nor free,*
> *Great nor servile, Lord, in Thee;*
> *Kindred love has all destroyed,*
> *Rendered all distinctions void,*
> *Names, and sects, and parties fall,*
> *Thou, O Christ, art All-in-all.*

## Self-Denying Hard Work

Increased access for Deaf people in church comes not from a vague detached theory or new theology, somehow presented on a plate. It comes from self-denying hard work, blueprinted in the pages of the Bible itself, and Deaf and hearing alike will need to roll up their sleeves and get stuck in.

**Note 1.** Some people criticise the healing of the Deaf man in *Mark 7*. They say that the Lord Jesus viewed the Deaf man as a medical problem only, which betrays His wrong attitude, much the same as most hearing people's wrong attitude toward Deaf people. This criticism is unfounded for the following reasons:

**a. The man wanted to become hearing.** He knew exactly what the Lord Jesus was doing, because He made sure the man understood, and he did not shrink from the healing.

**b. The man was a social outcast.** That was his biggest problem, not his Deafness. There was no government welfare department, and the culture of the day did not accept him. The Lord changed the man's social situation and made it possible for him to be fully accepted into society.

**c. Christ gave the man instant speech.** That was not a medical problem. The man had not learned to speak simply because he could not hear himself. The Lord accelerated the learning process into an instant in time, and the man spoke clearly.

**Note 2.** *Exodus 4:11*. This verse seems to say that God directly and deliberately creates disability. It is true that God is in control of everything, and also that people are born with all sorts of disabilities. Disability is part of a fallen world, marred by sin. Illness, disability, wars, suffering, etc., are all part of a world ruined by sin, and the Lord uses these situations to teach people the transient nature of the world. This is a Biblical view expounded in *Romans 8:22,* 'For we know that the whole creation groaneth and travaileth in pain together until now.' People should not set their hearts on riches and health and beauty, but they should seek spiritual riches through the Lord Jesus Christ.

As with all Scriptures, the context of a verse will aid the understanding of that verse. The context of *Exodus 4:11* is that God called Moses to do an important job. Moses doubted that he could do it. Moses thought that he didn't have the appropriate speech skills needed for the task. Maybe he worried that the people would not believe him or follow a man with a faltering voice. God reminded Moses that He can use anyone to serve Him, because God makes each person to fit a special place in His plan. God can call Deaf people to serve Him and does so. The verse teaches that God loves to fit people for His service, Deaf and hearing.

# NINE

# Digging Deeper
## A Challenge for Deaf People

How can we encourage Deaf Christians to take on more responsibility in the life of the church? Should the church be happy to give access and privilege but stop short of expecting something in return? Is the church doing enough? Is it possible to understand what makes Deaf people 'tick' as a key to understanding their needs and challenges in the church?

The old schoolmaster said, 'With privilege comes responsibility'. How true that is. Yet we see all around many famous people who indeed enjoy great privileges, but have not considered this motto. Celebrity scandal is there for all to see.

We have discussed the emergence of a new acceptance of Deafness on many fronts – in the media, in colleges and universities, in the workplace. Commentators have equated this with the civil rights struggle of black people in 1960s America, and the resulting statute-book equality. Certainly it was in the late 1970s and 1980s that an aggressive campaign was commenced in the UK for the rights of Deaf people. Some would say that the increasingly comfortable climate, and the acceptance of BSL as an official language, stems from those early struggles. Sure, Deaf people have rights. But what about responsibilities?

## The 'Support' Scenario

Deaf people are supported at every turn. Interpreters, social workers, friends they call on when they need to communicate. It is not uncommon now to see one Deaf student in an educational establishment with two communication support workers – one to interpret into BSL and the other to take notes, because the student cannot watch the communicator and take notes at the same time. Some people may be surprised at this. The fact is that Deaf people are supported, because language support is required. It means that a particular mindset develops and is reinforced through life.

Deaf people need language support in hearing churches. Interpreting is required and communication must take place. That is a basic need, and churches that understand this are happy to provide it. Some Deaf Christians, however, cannot conceive that they can take the initiative for themselves and be challenged by taking on responsibility. The 'support' scenario has done its work too thoroughly.

Are hearing Christians off the hook? No, many hearing Christians should feel a responsibility to take the initiative, but they simply don't want to. The Christian life is a warfare, or it should be. There should be battle against sin, and against the pressures of the world; the challenge of witness and making the gospel known should be addressed. There is work to be done. Sadly many ignore these responsibilities.

**The Christian life is a warfare, or it should be.**

What is the reward of taking it easy? That's it – an easy life. A life of ease, worldliness and pleasure. Nothing is hard. Labour for the Lord is out of fashion. The easy life is in, and the church becomes a social club. In some churches all the work is done by a small group of dedicated, 'spiritual soldiers', and the Lord blesses the church because of them and in spite of the others. The others freewheel, confident that someone else is doing the work. Their unspoken watchword is, 'Leave it to the Pastor, we pay him to do it.'

Deaf Christians have those pressures too, but alongside is the 'support' scenario: 'Why should I bother, I'm Deaf?' This is not a criticism of Deaf people. The bottom line is this – no one is exempt. All people saved by grace have responsibilities.

Churches therefore should have a ministry of encouragement and development, to bring Deaf people into the life of the church through service. Provide something to do, so Deaf people can serve the Lord.

The number of Deaf people going to church is relatively small. This is due, on a human level, to a combination of the following: the Deaf/hearing ratio in society; Deaf people's educational standards and low expectations; a lack of appropriate role models; a wrong attitude and a simple lack of access. On a spiritual level: the prejudice and love of the world that we all feel – Deaf and hearing – before we come to Christ, plus the devil keeping us in bondage to sin. Despite these barriers, by the grace of God, Deaf people do seek the Lord and are saved. Some find themselves amongst hearing believers in the local church. However, there is a recurring theme in the church: how seldom Deaf people are asked (or volunteer) to make a contribution, to take a lead and be responsible for carrying something through. We should try to address all this.

## Understanding the 'Deaf Psyche'

Let us consider the classic scenario. A church is confronted by the need to minister to Deaf people. At first it welcomes the opportunity, but sooner or later there is a clash of interests. Deaf people have needs, and they prefer those needs to be met in a 'Deaf way'. The church feels threatened because changes must be made. These changes, although quite reasonable to the Deaf mind, are hard for the hearing church leaders to swallow. They may feel uncomfortable because they perceive the very structure of their system of church authority is challenged, so a choice must be made: should the Deaf people be allowed to do things their way? – 'Leave them to it, they can use a room in the church for their meetings.' Or should the Deaf ministry be kept firmly within the body of the church, with its discipline and benefits? – 'We can find a way for them to adapt as comfortably as possible.'

How can we address this seeming polarisation? We need to step back and consider the 'Deaf psyche'. Who are Deaf people? What makes them tick? Are they simply people with a clinical hearing loss, or is there something else?

## Four Waves of Disadvantage

Deaf people feel little intrinsic disadvantage except when they mix with hearing people. We could identify four 'waves'. The first is the obvious loss of hearing in a hearing world. We have discussed that. The second is the disadvantage that comes through people's attitudes, and the non-inclusive nature of hearing society. That is clear, and we have discussed that also. There is a third wave, and it is important. It is best described as the dominant/dependant relationship. It could be that two people are close friends. They view each other as equals. They spend time with each other and know each other well. One is Deaf, the other hearing. Both use BSL fluently. Are they really equals? No – one is dominant, the other dependant. Which is which? The answer is clear. This third wave of disadvantage imparts a sort of inward burden, a sadness and negativity. This comes from all hearing people and their attitudes and prejudice, even close friends, because Deaf people depend on them as a language link. It conveys to Deaf people that they are judged to be inferior.

In our classic scenario, the church is on the back foot. They may want to provide benevolent help to Deaf people. The church believes that Deaf people are in need of help, so takes steps to provide it. This is a right, moral and Biblical duty, but it is also the problem. The hearing benevolent church decides what to do, and what help to give. Dominance and dependence occur. It may be unintended, but it is a fact of life. Deaf people may be grateful, but the help comes in the 'hearing' way. Deaf people would prefer the help to be given in the 'Deaf' way. They may ask for it repeatedly, but the hearing benefactors repeatedly misunderstand. Maybe not wilfully, but misunderstanding occurs. Or the benefactors regard the requests as nonsensical, whereas the Deaf people are deadly serious. The problem is that the help is essentially 'hearing/benevolent'.

## A Fourth Wave

The three waves are compounded further. Deaf people do not have direct access to the decision-makers in the church because they cannot communicate with them. The Deaf people have to go through an intermediary, a person who knows sign language. Such a person may know Deaf culture and ways well, so knows that the hearing decision-makers will not understand. The burden on that person is immense.

The intermediary may use one or more of the following coping strategies.

**1. Educate the decision-makers.** Every consultation will have a built-in set of backgrounds, motives and explanations as to why the Deaf people want such-and-such. The outcome may depend on how skilled the intermediary is in explaining the situation.

**2. Alter the Deaf requests.** The intermediary will submit a 'hearing' request to the decision-makers as a substitute for the 'Deaf' request, hoping that it will more readily be accepted, and that the Deaf people will be happy with the compromise.

**3. Educate the Deaf people.** The intermediary will explain to the Deaf people why the requests will not be understood or agreed to, except by way of compromise. The intermediary may recommend that a possible compromise should be asked for, and not the full-blown 'Deaf' request, because a compromise is more likely to succeed.

The outcome for each of these strategies is likely to be the same: the Deaf people will feel marginalised. There are more strategies, such as the 'do nothing and hope the problem will go away' option. Whatever strategy is adopted, the Deaf people will not feel fully satisfied.

## Do You Understand?

The 'Deaf psyche' is behind everything, but why is it so hard to understand? It may help to consider what happens to a Deaf child growing up.

Meet Mary, our fictitious Deaf person. She is born to hearing parents. From the start they do not fully understand her situation, having had no experience of what being Deaf means. They are therefore unable to identify important issues of awareness and needs. To simplify, there are six things that can be identified.

**1.** Communication and language development is restricted, compared to hearing children. Input from outside is patchy, unpredictable and often misunderstood. Her parents don't want to learn sign language. They want Mary to be like them, and try anything to achieve this.

**2.** Meeting other Deaf people is restricted, because her parents don't know any other Deaf people, and they don't realise how important it is for Mary to meet other Deaf people. This means that a peer group cannot develop, and role models are absent.

**3.** A specific Deaf identity is not accepted in everyday social interaction, and hearing people who interact with Mary are lacking in Deaf awareness and may be patronising.

**4.** The family has tensions which arise over Deaf issues, and this puts pressure on Mary. She is the problem, and she feels it. She is constantly pressured by hearing people to learn how to speak. Skilled speech and language therapists, doctors and audiologists are treating her, but she feels a failure because her hearing friends don't need to be treated. Her education suffers because so much time is spent on teaching her how to speak.

**5.** There is an absence of background noise and overheard conversations, and no one is filling in the gaps. No one can spare the time to explain what is going on. She cannot fathom the wants of others nor tell them her own.

**6.** Mary spends more and more time alone, so her sense of identity remains underdeveloped. She does not know where to belong. She is Deaf, feels constant pressure to be 'hearing', but is physically unable.

These all conspire together and stay with Mary through school years and beyond. They become part of her as a person. Indeed, the tensions she feels at home as a child are the same tensions she feels as an adult in the larger world. The baton is passed on, from school to college to employment, etc. Her childhood home situation turns out to be a microcosm of her adult life.

What is the end result? Mary seems to be very self-centred. All reference points are within, and she seems indifferent to the views or emotions of others. Also she feels that hearing people cannot understand, and they will always pressure for the 'hearing' way. When a hearing person tries to gently influence Mary, she feels pressure and answers, 'Don't force me!' All this affects relationships. Although Mary seeks out the company of Deaf people, it is sometimes hard to build and keep relationships. Fractures and niggles occur frequently, but they are quickly repaired because Mary needs other Deaf people. It seems to an outsider that relationships are there for mutual exploitation. All this may come as a big surprise to some people who view Deafness as just a medical condition.

Nowhere is the 'Deaf psyche' seen more clearly than around the table. Deaf guests at a meal will pile their plates high in case they miss something later. One man will take what he wants with no concept of assessing if there is enough to go round. One lady will put things in her bag to eat later. Another man will complain there is not enough food. Another lady thinks there is not enough cake, and will go to the shop. All these are real-life examples, and many Deaf people reading this will not see a problem. It's part of Deaf culture.

Are these things wrong? The cultural diversity of meal times is interesting: a guest from one culture may be surprised upon seeing someone clear the plate, because it indicates to them that more food is required. In another culture leaving food uneaten is an insult to the host. A loud belch may be the acceptable way of complimenting the chef. Who can judge between cultures?

At a church conference about Deaf issues, the speaker just prior to lunch made a 'Deaf joke' about making sure delegates went to the buffet in good time, because, 'Where Deaf people are, free food quickly disappears.' The man was himself Deaf.

## The 'Cycle Lane' Problem

The church is faced with a ministry to Deaf people. How can the church discharge its duty so that Deaf people feel truly comfortable and at ease?

On the London roads there is a network of cycle lanes. London boroughs are providing more and more safe routes for cyclists. There are cycling campaign organisations that put pressure on local authorities for change. Are things on the up for the London bike rider? No. Ask the average cyclist. Some cycle lanes go the long way round. Many are marked out on pavements, so cyclists have to mix with pedestrians and lamp posts, and they can't get up any speed. Often the cycle lane finishes abruptly – just when cyclists need a lane the most, where the road is narrower or there is danger. Cycles are allowed to use the bus lanes, but buses and cycles have different agendas. There is a green cycle-only area at the front of traffic light queues, but often cars and motorcycles illegally spill into it, revving up ready to go.

So we have opposite viewpoints. The authority believes it is doing a good job for cyclists, and cannot do any more. The cyclist says, 'It is not enough – there is much more that can be done.' Exactly the same scenario is being played out in churches. A church provides facilities for Deaf people: BSL interpreters, subtitles, print-outs of sermons, hymns projected, words pointed out and reserved seats. A budget is given for the use of the Deaf people – for food, transport, literature, etc. Someone is doing a huge amount of work for the Deaf people. But what do they say? 'It is not enough – there is much more that can be done.'

What is the answer to this 'cycle lane' problem? Churches must consider how far they want to go. One pastor has said that if he sees Deaf people signing in his entrance hall, unaware that the service time has arrived, he will wait and start the service late. On the other hand there can be great intolerance. A large group of Deaf people left the membership of a church because some hearing people made it quite clear that they didn't like the involuntary noises Deaf people made.

The cyclist's problem can be solved when the council leader understands because he is a cyclist himself, he has an unlimited budget for the roadway maintenance department, the department regards cycles as having equal importance as motor vehicles, and all drivers obey the law. Most of these are unlikely. It is the same for Deaf people in church. There is no quick fix or easy solution. This chapter is simply to help you be aware of the potential challenges that may be just around the corner. Clearly there must be compromise. As discussed before, integration is not the first priority for Deaf people, and it can be difficult for hearing people to understand and rise to the challenge. If you are a decision-maker in your church, how far you go is in your power. You must decide. But be assured that many hurdles will come.

It is important for the reader to understand that the things discussed in this chapter are generalisations, with the aim of providing insight. Churches will never be able to identify and seek to meet needs unless they can understand what the needs are. A challenge has been given to Deaf and hearing people. Deaf people are capable of unselfishness, open-heartedness, love and great patience, and we can labour with them in the work of the gospel.

**Note.** The June/July 2006 edition of the *London Cyclist* carried a report about cycle lanes:

'A strongly pro-cycling road safety officer was almost reduced to tears when he realised that instructors in his borough were discouraging the use of most of the network of cycle lanes for which he had campaigned for many years. However, after taking some National Standard lessons he reluctantly agreed that in many cases cyclists using the lanes were at greater risk than cyclists who chose not to use them.'

This has a ring of truth about it for Deaf worshippers in many churches. Well-meaning church leaders may try to give Deaf worshippers what they think they need, without researching or considering possible alternatives which would suit them better. The result of such uninformed benevolence may be that Deaf people will look for another church.

## TEN

# Parents of Deaf Children

**M**y baby has recently been diagnosed as Deaf. What shall I do? How can I communicate with my baby? What about school? Is there an operation that can help? How can I find other families in the same situation?

Parents who discover their child is Deaf may experience great shock. Their way of coping will be to try to make their child the same as a hearing child – they will want the child to use speech and have oral/written English as their first language. They will certainly feel great frustration with communication. They may decide that their child should be taught to lipread at all costs. They will find that advice comes from many sides and is conflicting. They will be confused and not know what is for the best.

Parents should seek help from as many sources as possible, Deaf people included. For every strongly held view there is an equally adamantly held alternative. Knowing all the options and outcomes will help them decide the way forward.

## Deaf Parents of Hearing Children

Only 10% of Deaf children are born to Deaf parents. Deaf parents who have a Deaf baby will know what to expect, and will communicate naturally from the start. They will accept their child readily, feel no shock or worry, and the child will have British Sign Language as a first language. The critical objective then is to give the child a grasp of written English, because that is the basic tool of communication between the hearing and Deaf.

It is more common for Deaf parents to have hearing children. Many people are surprised to learn that some Deaf parents with hearing children experience the same emotions as hearing parents with deaf children: disappointment, shock, worry. Sometimes hearing children of Deaf parents learn to speak only when old enough to go to school, because no speech is used at home. The child will grow up to be naturally bilingual, and the parents will rely on the child for communication. The child may be called upon to interpret in situations far beyond his or her years. For example, a school has a Parents' Evening. The school knows that Johnny's parents are Deaf but has failed to book an interpreter. Johnny therefore becomes the interpreter, but is also under discussion.

## Signing with my Baby?

If hearing parents decide that communication via sign language with their Deaf child is preferred, it will be a race to learn BSL quickly enough to be able to teach it naturally to the child, in the same way as a hearing family will teach a hearing child to speak. Parents will find that advice and practical help from Deaf BSL users is essential.

Many Deaf children live in families that cannot sign. They use notes, or their own developed gestures. The family cannot fully include the Deaf child in all that goes on. The child misses what people are saying, and why they are doing things – just those normal little 'chats' amongst families. Maybe the Deaf child has seen people in the family having a row, but no one explains what has happened. The parents may not have time to explain why, or indeed want to. The hearing child understands what is going on just by overhearing, but the Deaf child misses out on the natural everyday things that others take for granted. The Deaf child feels isolated. The parents are neglecting to learn a language to use as they bring up the child. They may in effect be neglecting that child.

## What about Education?

To answer this question we must first be aware of the different methods of education used with children who are Deaf. From just before the 20th century, Deaf children were almost exclusively taught in the oral way, in dedicated schools for Deaf children. They were taught how to speak with an emphasis on English. This was because of an ill-fated congress in Milan in 1880.

At this congress, a declaration was made that the oral method of education was superior to that of using sign language. Eight resolutions in favour of the oral method of education over the sign language method were passed with high majorities, giving those who opposed the resolutions no opportunity to prevent them being passed. The congress was cited as an 'enormous success', and a cruel wave of 'oralism' began to permeate the education system of many countries. Because of the Milan Congress, schools discarded educating Deaf children through sign language, and academic achievement was measured by a child's lipreading skills, and on leaving school, how well a child could make him/herself understood by using a spoken voice.

That meant that they were not allowed to sign, and corporal punishment was used if they were caught doing so. Despite that, they signed in the playground and outside school. There are many Deaf adults today who can give bitter witness to how education marginalised their language, and look back on their school experience with disdain.

Such strict methods used in schools have passed from fashion. There are still dedicated schools for Deaf children in Britain today, but the numbers are declining. These are specialist schools that promote a variety of teaching techniques. To summarise, some teach in BSL, some orally, others in total communication, which is a mixture of signing, speaking and lipreading – in other words, all the available methods of communication. If a child shows that he or she can benefit through using hearing and speaking, that is encouraged; if BSL, then that is emphasised. As these schools are few, the child may need to travel far to attend, and parents may need to campaign for their child to attend the most appropriate school.

A Deaf person's school has an immense influence in his or her life for many years after childhood, far more than a hearing person's. It is not uncommon for Deaf adults meeting for the first time to ask each other what school they went to, before they ask each other their names.

Deaf children now are increasingly placed in mainstream schools, or in 'units' in a school, but the quality of education is not nationally consistent, because it can depend on the attitudes of teaching staff. Also, there may or may not be specialist Teachers of Deaf children (ToD) in residence at the school, because the budget may only support a peripatetic ToD. That being said, the aim of such units is to integrate the child into the full social and learning environment. The mainstream or Deaf-only education issue is much debated amongst Deaf people and educationalists alike.

## The Parents' Dilemma

A Deaf child is born to hearing parents. The parents have no idea of the Deaf world of language and culture. Their child is born into the hearing world. They naturally want that child to grow up to be part of their world. The choice of education may reflect that desire. As that child grows it will become obvious that there is a profound choice to be made. That choice is between the Deaf and the hearing worlds.

A friend of ours was fifteen before she met another person who wore hearing aids like her. It was the most amazing thing that had happened to her. Here was someone else who had gone through the trauma of being ignored because she could not hear properly. Here was someone else who had been laughed at because of what she wore on her ears. Here was someone else who understood. For fifteen years her parents had not realised the importance of bringing their child into contact with others like her.

Some parents of Deaf children will attempt at all costs to keep their child away from other Deaf people and from sign language. It could be because they know they would have to learn sign language themselves, or maybe it is because they fear they may lose their child to the Deaf world. (Their child will probably join the Deaf world on becoming an adult anyway.) It is a fear of the unknown. However, some parents are well aware of the issues, and they want to give their

**Having a language is a cornerstone with which to learn another language.**

child initially a good grounding in the hearing world of education, with its English grammar, so different from the grammar of BSL. Later, perhaps, they will introduce sign language. Some feel it is important to give their child a full, rounded education and opt for both. Parents naturally want the best for their child.

An important consideration is that having a language is a cornerstone with which to learn another language. Because of this, parents should not fear to introduce their child to signing, or to start learning signing themselves, because communication is the important thing. Teaching English to a child who already has language (sign or any other) is easier than teaching a child who has no language at all.

## Cochlear Implants

There is another alternative for parents, and some will have availed themselves of this option. Their child has had a surgical procedure, which has placed an electrode array into the inner ear and given the child a form of hearing.

Implants work as follows. A small microphone picks up

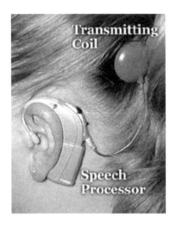

sound. A speech processor digitises the sounds into coded signals. These signals are sent to a transmitting coil, which is positioned at the side of the head, held there magnetically. An embedded receiver (placed surgically just underneath the skin behind the ear) picks up these signals and sends them to an electrode array, placed by surgery in the fluid of the inner ear. The auditory nerve sends the electrical signal to the brain in the normal way just like a healthy ear does. What the brain 'hears' is not a natural sound, but a sort of mechanical 'Dalek' noise, which needs to be learned afresh by the brain.

Implants are an emotive subject in the Deaf world, for a variety of reasons. Critics cite the following: the procedure destroys all vestigial hearing, surgery is not 100% successful and is expensive, the procedure and appliances continue to be experimental, there is very patchy research about the success of hearing and improvement in speech. Adults can choose for themselves whether to have a cochlear implant, but young children cannot – their parents must make the choice for them. Most Deaf people say the child should be given the opportunity to grow and develop a personality, and understand the issues before making such a personal choice. This is one of what seems like an endless array of profound, life-altering decisions that must be made by parents of Deaf children. It is a monumental responsibility, and the child cannot normally make the decision for himself or herself.

Having an implant has transformed many lives. It has allowed people to continue a career, be socially confident and aware of environmental sounds, even some speech. The great majority of these people are adults who have lost their hearing, and have had an implant to restore the hearing they once had.

We cannot enter the debate here, as parents must make the decision in an informed way with health, audiology and educational professionals, with others who can advise from experience, and with Deaf people themselves. It is a sad situation, however, that advice from the Deaf community is rarely sought, usually because (a) parents may not understand the importance of seeking it, and may not know how to seek it, and (b) health professionals may not suggest they do so.

## Deaf Children and Mental Health

The proportion of Deaf children with diagnosed mental health needs is much higher than in a comparable population of hearing children. It is a sad fact that a percentage are mis-diagnosed due to poor identification of Deaf behavioural traits; but putting that to one side, this high proportion springs from poor communication and the isolation it causes (as well as the bullying, abuse and other problems that many Deaf children experience). This surely is an incentive for parents to begin to sign with their child as early as possible.

All children, Deaf and hearing, live in a juvenile make-believe world which forgives the lack of adult intervention, simply because the child is not particularly interested in it. That make-believe world acts like a sort of buffer to many of the griefs which adults are crushed by. However, we must not take this for granted. Children must get access to good communication early on. That alone is a good motivation for a Sunday School. In the next chapter we will look in more detail at the importance of Deaf children attending Sunday School.

## Help for Parents

The **National Deaf Children's Society** is the only UK charity solely dedicated to providing support, information and advice for Deaf children and young people, their families and the professionals working with them. Their contact details are in the Appendix.

ELEVEN

# The Children's Sunday School

What do we need to consider when approaching the needs of Deaf children? Are there special methods we must use? Should we target the Deaf children in our neighbourhood, or try to provide facilities if they come in? How do we teach?

There are approximately 23,000 Deaf children under the age of 16 in the UK. The vast majority are born to hearing parents. This means that all those sets of parents have to go through the same learning curve, and have to make big choices early on which will affect the growing child well into adulthood.

Siblings will not necessarily feel the need to communicate. During a family holiday in France, we stayed near a farm with French children of the same age as ours. We attempted to communicate with the adults, and enjoyed the experience, but the children played happily for hours without uttering a word to each other.

## Signs or Words?

What is the extent of the hearing loss? Will the child be sent to a specialist or mainstream school? Will the child be required to speak and learn English at all costs? Will the parents learn sign language as quickly as possible and begin to communicate in that way early on?

It may be that a child comes into Sunday School who is learning to live with a cochlear implant, as discussed in the previous chapter. That child may need sign language to support the learning process, and may be learning to lipread also. Being aware will help communication.

When considering a ministry for Deaf children as part of the Sunday School, we would do well to try and understand something about Deaf education (see previous chapter) because we need to think about where the child and the parents are potentially coming from. There may well be hidden issues to consider. You should not simply ask one of your teachers to learn sign language quickly with the aim of teaching that child. It may actually take someone two or three years to learn adequately to do that, but even then you will be faced with the situation that the child knows more BSL than the teacher, because even a Deaf child of three years can be remarkably fluent.

Be aware that parents may have an agenda, such as not wishing their child to be exposed to sign language. The parents will be sure to let you know if they have, so try to meet the parents as soon as possible to sort things out. It will be comforting to them that you are aware of the issues. It may be that the parents have no fear of sign language. Then you may go ahead, but remember there are other forms of communication and employ them.

The most important thing is not to assume you know the best thing to do, and how the child should be taught, without understanding the issues. Do not present the parents with 'This is what we will do for your child.' Consultation and understanding are vital. Take time to discuss and decide a way forward, then stick to it.

# A Deaf Child Appears in Sunday School

You have not been expecting this little girl. She sits with the friend who brought her. She doesn't sing with the others, but some children don't anyway. You ask her name, and her friend tells you. She sits in class with the others, but doesn't ask any questions. You are busy with the ones that do, anyway. She goes home. You are unaware she is Deaf.

This is a true-life scenario. Such a Deaf child may have learned something, but probably not much. It is essential you pick up the reality of the situation early, and take steps to deal with it. Who in the Sunday School can teach such a child?

There may be Deaf children in your neighbourhood who will one day walk into the Sunday School, but equally there may be parents of a Deaf child who would be willing to send that child to Sunday School if they knew there was one nearby that catered for Deaf children.

The best teacher for a Deaf child is a Deaf teacher. The child will know the teacher is Deaf and will respond. The

**The best teacher for a Deaf child is a Deaf teacher.**

teacher will be aware of all the emotions and frustrations of the child. There will be a meeting of minds that will lower barriers to the gospel message.

The first Deaf child who came into our Sunday School wanted to be the same as the other children. He came with his cousin and sat in class with the hearing boys and felt comfortable. He held up songs at the front like the hearing children, and helped with the offering.

Then we asked one of our Deaf members to teach him. The boy at first resisted. He was in a class of two – him and the teacher. He thought he was being treated differently because of his Deafness, but very quickly that changed. Later on one or two other Deaf adults sat in and made it a little group. He felt more at home because of that, and when the others were not able to be there he missed them and asked where they were.

It may be you do not have anyone who is Deaf who can teach in Sunday School. If so, a hearing teacher must. Someone who is fluent in sign language can sign and speak at the same time (when that is done, Sign Supported English must be used) so that Deaf and hearing children can both understand. It is, however, possible to teach without any sign language.

## Teaching without Sign Language

Think about this scenario. You have no sign language at all, and meet a Deaf person who cannot lipread. You both want to communicate. What do you do?

1. You go through your pockets for a pen and paper. The written word is in the Deaf person's second language, and your first, so there is an immediate communication link of sorts.

2. You have no pen or paper, so you write letters in the air, or on your hand.

3. You gesticulate. Hearing people do this without thinking. How do you ask the waiter across a noisy restaurant for the bill? Have you ever wagged your finger at someone in reproach? Do you have a gesture for 'telephone'?

4. You point, maybe at a picture, or draw a picture.

So you have four methods. A good Sunday School teacher will have a stock of pictures and headings. Notes written as the lesson proceeds will aid communication. Gesticulation is very powerful. Your fingers can become a walking figure. You can open an imaginary door, or look through an imaginary window. Try and explain the woman sweeping the house for her lost coin, or Abraham raising his blade over Isaac, or Goliath walking out from the Philistine ranks with his massive armour and weapons – all using gesture.

You will have to assess, though, if the whole class is generally learning less as you concentrate on perhaps one member of the class; or you may feel you could teach the Deaf child more efficiently without the hearing members of your class being there. It opens up the debate about integration or dedication (discussed in chapter 5).

## Not Just Teaching a Story

What about the application of the lesson? The narrative is the easy bit – but how do you apply the meaning and challenge the child? Suppose the lesson next Sunday is the parable of the Good Samaritan from *Luke 10:25-37.* You can explain the narrative, but the real need is to challenge the children. You want to get across that life is like a journey, but it is dangerous. You want to show how the attack of the robbers is a picture of us being attacked by all kinds of evil in this world. You plan to demonstrate that the wounded Jew stands for how this world takes everything from us and leaves us broken and dying, heading for hell. You want to equate the Scribe and Pharisee who passed by, to those worldly crutches we turn to through life to give us hope, but which have nothing to offer those who are in great spiritual need. You want them to understand that our help comes from an unexpected source, like the Samaritan who helped his enemy. 'For when we were yet without strength...Christ died for the ungodly' *(Romans 5:6).* You intend prayerfully to press home a challenge to turn to the Saviour. You are wrestling with the hearing children to get across these vital points. How can you do so with the Deaf children? It is a dilemma that is very strongly linked to the integration or dedication question.

## Integration in the Sunday School

A Deaf Sunday School teacher may advise a method of teaching Deaf children which is different from that used to teach hearing children, because if we teach a lesson which is

English-based to children whose first language is not English, much of the information is lost. One way is to proceed slowly, bit by bit, teasing out the lesson in small chunks. That may be a problem – the Sunday School has a curriculum. Each Sunday there is a new lesson with a new challenge, a fresh way of pointing the children to Christ. Each lesson is packed with narrative and applications and vital spiritual meanings. It is too much. The details of the narrative will drown the spiritual meaning. Maybe the Deaf child should be taught a targeted lesson over a number of weeks, so meaning is made clear; but that means that Deaf and hearing cannot proceed together in the curriculum. Also it may be boring for the Deaf children to see the same pictures and learn about the same characters week by week. It will also fuel the negative feeling that Deaf children are 'different', when they see other children speeding ahead with new lessons and pictures.

One answer is to follow the curriculum, but pick out just one or two major applications to press home. That may be one method, but Deaf children and their communication needs are varied. Some will be OK with an interpreter, some will have partial hearing and will lipread, some will be good with English.

However we teach in Sunday School, to Deaf or hearing, one vital principle applies: the gospel call must be faithfully and clearly given week after week without fail.

## The Challenge of the Gospel

We must not waste precious time with colouring pictures and activities. They can be done at home. The short hour on Sunday afternoon is critical, and could mean the difference between Heaven and hell. The Sunday School teacher is possibly the only source of contact for the gospel the child has. The Deaf child is no exception. We must not give colouring to

Deaf children just because that may be the easiest way to occupy them. The gospel must be presented to all, because all are desperately in need of it.

If your Sunday School is one that has activities, play and colouring, etc., how can the hearing children see through it all and understand the doctrine of the gospel and be challenged? The Deaf child has even less opportunity.

You may think this is a hobbyhorse for old-fashioned Sunday Schooling. Well, think about this: you are a Deaf child. You come to Sunday School as usual, and sit there. Any speech is unheard. The music of the songs means nothing. You may have the words of the song pointed out to you, but not explained. The words are complicated, and they are quickly forgotten because there is no tune to run through your head to hang them on. A teacher speaks, but another child who has brought a toy to Sunday School diverts your eyes. Unlike the hearing children, you cannot hear the teacher whilst looking at something else, even if you have an interpreter there. Communication is through the eyes. The teaching style is free and relaxed, so there is much to divert your eyes. A teacher speaks about the Bible, then some pictures are used. Now you are getting somewhere: something to look at, pictures of people doing this and that, but you don't know who they are. The teacher waves her hands, but not in sign language. The teacher puts up some words on the pictures. So now you have a further clue, but that's all you have – clue after clue. You are constantly putting bits and pieces together, guessing and conjecturing what it all means, and there is such a lot of other visual activity going on which is far more interesting and easier to grasp. Even with an interpreter there, you have to concentrate to see what is being said. But no one else seems to be concentrating. Your mind wanders. Then you realise it is

**That's all you have – clue after clue.**

time for an activity, because the other children are moving their chairs around. The colouring pens come out. Sheets are given, and the activity begins. You enjoy it, because there is interaction between all the children, asking for different coloured pens and copying each other. The time flashes by and it is time for home.

You had a good time, but you go home unaware of the most important thing you could ever know, that the Lord Jesus suffered and died and made atonement for sin – possibly *your* sin piled up high through even your few years of selfishness, pride and deceit. You are unaware, and it is the fault of the Sunday School and the teacher.

## The Old-Fashioned Gospel

Someone once asked, 'How can you seriously expect to keep a class of (hearing) children quiet for 25 minutes while you teach, without using activities?' There is an answer, but not an easy one. It means hard work and dedication. There are two basic ways to get that atmosphere of learning required to support a quiet class of Sunday School children.

First of all it starts in the very youngest class, when children come in as toddlers. It is there that an atmosphere is set and maintained. Then as the children grow through the Sunday School, they take it with them. New children coming in at a later age are more likely to conform to the prevailing atmosphere.

Secondly, and this is perhaps more important, the teacher must hold the class with such interest and discipline that the children are transfixed. There is no easy answer.

We must have structure and ground rules when working with children. Some come from broken homes, and have only one adult caring for them. Many do not have a father to provide masculine stability. The Sunday School teacher must seek to give that stability. The Deaf child in the class is one step further away than the hearing child in terms of communication, so stability is even more important. Structure is the only platform from which the truths of God's Word can be adequately taught. Provide some colouring to do at home, yes, but in the Sunday School engage directly with the soul.

## TWELVE

# Planning for the Future
### 15 Things for You to Do

How do I start a ministry for Deaf people? What practical issues should I consider? Must it be a department of the church, or an independent organisation? What are my aims in starting a Deaf ministry?

If you have no ministry for Deaf people in your church but are considering one, there are some very practical issues that must be addressed, and there are many things to do. The following are not listed in order of priority.

## 1. Identify the Purpose

It seems an obvious thing to say, but any department of the church should exist to be evangelistic. The Sunday School, the women's meeting, the older folk's gathering, the toddlers' group are all first and foremost evangelistic. Many churches have lost sight of this. The Deaf ministry should be no exception to this rule. Having a ministry for Deaf believers only will be doomed to failure. The aim will be insular, the attitude to visiting Deaf unbelievers will be frosty, and the Deaf people of your neighbourhood will remain unreached. There must be a positive campaign to reach people for Christ. The apostle Paul said in *1 Corinthians 9:16*, 'For necessity is laid upon me;

yea, woe is unto me, if I preach not the gospel!' Then later he exhorted his friend in *2 Timothy 3:10, 11, 14; 4:1, 2* to follow his example. That exhortation is a command from Paul as God's inspired example to Timothy, and the pattern for all the churches in this gospel age, before the Saviour comes again, so it is binding on us as well as Timothy. The gospel must be declared in every department of the church. Indeed, we should start with the gospel, and consider what departments of the church we can use to declare it.

**The gospel must be declared in every department of the church.**

There must also be a Bible study for Deaf Christians. Believers must be instructed and built up, and worship must take place. The pastor must be enlisted. He should be the driving force of the initiative. He can motivate the church, and by his positive attitude will lead by example. But it must be done within the church. Starting a Deaf work independently from the church is not advisable. Today there are many societies run by earnest believers, doing good works, but independent from any local church direction. That some such societies sprang out of church lethargy is well known, but we must strive to conform to the New Testament blueprint.

## 2. Choose a Leader

The best leader of a Deaf department of the church is a Deaf Christian. That person will know all the reasons why things are done in a particular way, and will be part of Deaf culture. Deaf people who come in will feel at home, and that person can lead with confidence. That person will know other Deaf people, and will be readily accepted in local Deaf situations. If there is no suitable Deaf believer to lead, then a hearing person will have to take up the gauntlet, but that person must be aware of certain fundamental Deaf issues, and be patient, because there will be no meteoric success.

It may take some time for a hearing person to be accepted and trusted in the Deaf world, for reasons discussed earlier. Patience must be exercised. In time, barriers will be broken down and friendships forged, but a long-term prayerful commitment is required.

A hearing person can easily blunder into the Deaf world and cause offence. If a Deaf person feels he or she is being forced into something by a well-meaning but condescending hearing person, a fracture may occur. If an important Deaf cultural issue is being overlooked without an attempt to understand, there may be offence. As a result, Deaf people can become introverted and wary. Counselling between hearing and Deaf, therefore, may be slow and fragmented, and will certainly require an eagerness to understand. Deaf people are a true cross-section of the community – male and female, young and old, all differing shades of intellect, the same as hearing people. Deafness is their common link, and only Deaf people can truly 'understand' each other. Pastoral counselling of Deaf people by Deaf people therefore is the ideal (whether the Deaf person is capable or called to counsel is obviously to be addressed first), but a hearing person who is aware of the issues can be accepted and trusted in time, and so fulfil the role.

> **A hearing person can easily blunder into the Deaf world and cause offence.**

## 3. Be Aware of Very Practical Issues

There are many considerations. Deaf people take longer to do things. For instance, mealtimes are longer. When you are sitting next to a Deaf friend at the table, enjoying a meal, you will naturally feel the need to communicate. You will discover that you cannot eat and sign at the same time. You may think it will be easy, because you are not actually using your mouth to

119

**But be ye doers of the word, and not hearers only (James 1:22)**

speak, but the opposite is true. You will need to concentrate on the signs with your entire eye-gaze. This means you cannot glance down to load your fork with food. And when you sign, it's impossible to use your hands for anything but signing. You may be hungry, but you cannot divert your gaze without breaking the flow of signs, or appearing to be uninterested in the signer. The meal takes longer, and hearing people at the table have finished long ago. A buffet meal is problematic, for the obvious reason that you have to hold a plate. When you want to discuss many things, then leave the meal for another time, or choose a cold dish.

It is easier to sign with someone sitting opposite you, so if you invite two Deaf people for a meal, don't sit them together. Deaf people will often ignore the person next to them, and sign with someone who may actually be out of comfortable talking distance for a hearing person. A large square table is better than a long thin one.

The writer was once in a group of Deaf people walking along a river embankment. Progress was slow, and potentially dangerous, because concentrating on each other's signing and looking where you are going at the same time is difficult. There was a noise, and the hearing people looked to see the trainer of a rowing club cycling along the path, shouting orders at the rowers in the water. The Deaf people were all unaware. Then a number of hungry swans on the river started following our group along the bank. A quaint picture, but all unnoticed because of the desire to communicate.

These scenarios serve to illustrate that there is such a thing as 'Deaf time', because the need to communicate is so strong that everything else takes a secondary place, including time. Also it is 'Deaf culture', as discussed before, that compels people to travel miles to find a dedicated Deaf meeting, and with the vagaries of travel, people will turn up very early, and more often, very late. After an afternoon Deaf meeting, which finished at 5pm, we had cleared up and were leaving at about 7.30pm, when a Deaf lady arrived for the meeting. We have also had experience of Deaf people turning up as early as 4.30pm for an evening meeting starting at 7pm!

Expect Deaf people to arrive at odd times, and leave plenty of time for everything. Hearing people must fit into the Deaf way of doing things, and not expect Deaf people to conform to the hearing way, because it is practically not an option. Hurrying Deaf people along at breakneck speed is not comfortable for them. Making sure things are ready at the time stated is the leader's responsibility, but the leader must be patient when things turn out differently. If you start a campaign to train Deaf people into hearing ways, then you will be disappointed. Expect the unexpected, and don't take it personally if disappointments occur.

## 4. Form Friendships

In a church where Deaf people attend, some hearing people will naturally come forward and show their interest and attempt to communicate. Encourage this. Find out details of a sign language course and make it known. If your signing is patchy and you have booked an interpreter, then get those interested people to come forward to use the interpreter to communicate before and after the service. Make the Deaf people feel welcome in the fellowship. A warm smile of greeting is an easy thing to do. If there is anything that the Deaf people can help with in the church, then make sure you ask them. It could be to start a programme of teaching sign language in the church. Do not exclude them from anything, even when communication is inadequate. With more contact, Deaf people will feel more at home, hearing people will learn how to communicate, and friendships will be formed.

## 5. Keep in Touch

Some hearing people are amused by the fact that Deaf people have mobile phones. This is not surprising when you consider the popularity of SMS (small message sending, or 'texting'). This is a good way to keep in touch with Deaf friends. SMS has largely taken over from the old-fashioned minicom, or textphone (a telephone that has a keyboard for typing messages to another user). However, these textphones are still very much in use. If you know someone who has a textphone, it is possible to communicate from a regular phone via a dedicated exchange in Liverpool. This service is called RNID Typetalk. It is provided jointly by the RNID and BT. You ring the exchange with 18002 then the number of the textphone you want to contact. An operator will come on the line and type your side of the conversation, which comes up on the textphone display of the person you are calling. The operator will tell you what the textphone user is typing in reply. Textphone users dial 18001 then the number of the person they would like to speak to, and the operator joins the line and proceeds in the same way. There are hundreds of public textphones in the UK provided by RNID Typetalk.

Videophones are available. They are expensive, but prices are falling. Many Deaf people have fax machines at home. These are fairly inexpensive, and can be set up to come on automatically if another fax machine is calling. A fax machine is a good investment if you would like Deaf people to be able to contact you easily. Many interpreters and communicators have fax machines. Then there are PC cams, used over the internet. Also E-mail is an obvious way to keep in touch.

## 6. Arrange the Furniture

Don't assume that the seating arrangements should be the same as at a hearing meeting. For a Deaf-only meeting the arrangement of seats is an important consideration. Rows of seats with people sitting behind each other are not ideal, because the line of sight is critical. (In a worst-case scenario, a hearing person can hear a preacher when sitting behind a pillar.) For a small group of Deaf people, a circle of seats is best. Everyone has a clear view, and it is easier to keep together during a hymn.

## 7. Consider the Integrated or Dedicated Question

This was discussed earlier (see chapter 5) but what is practical? Both integrated and dedicated, if possible, although it may not be easy. The church may be set in a rural environment. There may not be any Deaf people living nearby who can come regularly to the Sunday services, but a dedicated meeting once a month would be eminently feasible. As discussed before, Deaf people will travel miles to be with one another. A meeting with time to chat, possibly a meal, and a direct gospel 'epilogue' or a sermon to finish may well draw people in. Be aware of the days and times of local Deaf clubs, and work round them. Indeed, visit these clubs and ask if you can put up a poster on their notice board. Print out a newsletter and advertise a forthcoming preaching topic that may interest Deaf people. Organise special outings from time to time. Enlist the help of hearing people for driving, preparing meals and generally helping out.

If you start to learn BSL, then Deaf contacts will be made. In time your circle of Deaf acquaintances will grow and you can invite them in.

If none of these things brings people in, consider trying to get Deaf children into the Sunday School. Don't, however, think of this as an alternative only. Aiming to bring the gospel to Deaf children is absolutely vital.

If Deaf people are integrated with the main hearing services of your church, you will need to be aware of certain practical issues such as hymn singing, discussed before. Seating arrangements may have to be altered. People may need to be enlisted as notetakers or as typists, and the words projected. An interpreter should be found. All these things have been discussed earlier. But there are also some considerations for the pulpit.

## 8. Brief the Preacher

Put yourself for a moment in the interpreter's shoes: you arrive for the morning service. The minister has given you the text for the sermon, but that is all. (Incidentally, there are stories of interpreters patrolling the pavement outside churches hoping to catch the minister when he arrives to obtain a clue of what he will be speaking on.) The church uses the beautiful *Authorised Version,* but it is a fact of life that most Deaf people simply cannot understand it. You must translate from the English of the King James Bible into 21st century BSL, but how do you do it? You will probably have a carefully chosen modern version with you, to aid the process. There are versions of the Bible specifically published for Deaf people, and you probably have a copy with you, because it is not simply a matter of signing word for word. Replacing unfamiliar, complicated words with simple everyday signs must happen. (See note at the end of this chapter.) In practice, that contorted process of hearing, understanding, replacing and signing can be compounded and turned into a nightmare.

The morning service is under way. The preacher announces a Scripture verse during the flow of the sermon, to make a point clear. You have no prior warning of the verse. The hearing people locate the verse quickly in their own Bibles and are ready to read with the minister. He may start to read the verse while they are looking it up. That's OK because, unlike

Deaf people, they can listen as they search. The Deaf worshippers have to wait for you to interpret to them the Scripture reference – they are lagging behind the hearing congregation already. You then have to look up the reference in your own modern translation before signing the verse, unless you wait until the preacher reads it, and then interpret it from the English that is read out. But you cannot do that because the Deaf people are still head-down looking up the verse and reading it. They may read English more slowly than hearing people, because it is their second language. You cannot continue until their eye-gaze lifts towards you. By then the preacher is well into the explanation of the verse, or may have moved on to his next reference. Proof texts flow thick and fast. You gulp and rapidly interpret into BSL. But then the preacher picks out a word in a verse and explains the Greek meaning. You have to backtrack, fingerspell the word, which may be unintelligible to Deaf people, then explain its meaning as given by the preacher. You must therefore, because of the necessary time constraints, clip some of the information, or indicate that the Deaf people need not look up the Scripture, because you will sign it for them. Inevitably some editing of the material must take place. The Deaf people miss out, and you have an uncomfortable time.

This is not a call to ministers to change the Bible version they use. It is simply a request to be aware of the difficulties faced by interpreters. The most important key to better interpreting is being forearmed. This is the same for all interpreting the world over. Interpreters who are consistently given little information before assignments may well decline future ones, and given the shortage of interpreters, it is important for preachers to address the issue. With prior warning meanings will be made clearer, Deaf people will keep up with the worship, and the interpreter will be more confident and happy that a good job has been done. All this is in the hands of the preacher.

Sometimes it is impossible to think so far ahead. It may be impossible to change the habits of a lifetime. If for any reason this information cannot be obtained before the minister ascends the pulpit steps, if he is aware of the problems and allows a few precious seconds at vital points in the sermon, it will help immensely. A measure of Deaf awareness will go a long way.

To help you understand, quickly replace each of the following words with a simpler word or phrase: ascension, manifested, forerunner, dimension, instrumentality. An interpreter has to do this instantly during the flow of a sermon.

## 9. Be Aware of Social Interaction

Despite the cheerfulness of a hearing person's involvement with Deaf people there may be hidden issues. We've all had the experience of being in a room where two young people are glancing around, whispering and giggling with each other. Their enjoyment is plain to see, and they may be talking about innocent teenage things. Unfortunately, everyone else in the room thinks they are talking about them. It is a natural reaction. So imagine a room of Deaf and hearing people. Two hearing people are talking and glancing toward a Deaf person now and again, and that person notices. What are they to think? When there are only Deaf people in a room, everyone can see what everyone else is saying. There is no whispering with sign language. When Deaf people sign, anyone can eavesdrop, and it is not rude to do so. That is one reason why Deaf people can be brutally honest with each other, because it is difficult to hide interaction. Hearing people should be aware of this. Do not talk confidentially about Deaf people when they are there. Some are very good at lipreading. They may ask you what you are saying, and you might feel your cheeks flushing as a result. When Deaf people are around be careful to sign as you speak with another hearing person if you can. It is only right to include everyone in the conversation, especially if you are talking about Deaf things. Not all Deaf people will assume that your conversation is benign, and the fact that you are talking and omitting to sign may imply that you don't want them to hear.

## 10. Protect Personal Safety

Parents of young Deaf people are understandably nervous about their offspring travelling alone, especially returning on a late evening in the dark. In some areas this is risky for hearing people, and a young Deaf woman, for instance, is more vulnerable than most. Being unaware of noises that would warn hearing people of danger is a distinct disadvantage. You should be concerned for their safety also. It may be that you will need to arrange a lift from a member of your church who lives near the Deaf person. In that way you and any relatives will be assured of personal safety, and it could be the facility that allows the Deaf person to come to church at all. Offering a lift to church means that the person is more likely to arrive at the right time for the service.

## 11. Promote Deaf Awareness Training

Many colleges provide Deaf awareness courses. Indeed, some will not accept people on a BSL course without them first having a Deaf awareness qualification, or at least be taking a concurrent course with BSL. This is an absolute must for anyone wishing to work with Deaf people in a ministry of the church, and an excellent idea for members of a church with Deaf people attending. In fact, it may be possible to arrange for a Deaf awareness teacher to come and take a class in the church itself, leading to an exam and qualification. Many people regard Deaf awareness training as not essential, but it remains true that a course of this nature is interesting, enlightening and of great practical value.

## 12. Use the Right Terms

In the past, Deaf people have been labelled in various ways, which today can cause offence. We need to know what is acceptable today, especially if we want to produce a newsletter or magazine for Deaf people in our neighbourhood. Do not use the label 'the Deaf', but rather use the phrase 'Deaf people', 'hard of hearing people' or 'people with a hearing loss'. Never use the terms 'Deaf and dumb' or 'Deaf mute'. These are offensive and inaccurate. Do not describe Deaf people as 'suffering from hearing loss', or as being 'victims'. This can give Deaf people a negative view of your attitude toward them, and negatively influence others.

When referring to Deaf people in church magazines and written material, use the capital D as in 'Deaf people', rather than 'deaf people'. For those new to the Deaf world, this can look strained and 'politically correct', but if this convention is not followed some Deaf people may feel offended. Some will be wary and stay away, thinking that your church is not Deaf-aware. There are publications that get over this confusion by using the term 'D/deaf people'. This may be making too much of the issue. If in doubt, use the capital D. To address this confusion, the word 'Deaf' with a capital letter is used throughout this book.

## 13. Spend Some Money

Deaf people will flock to a free meal. Many Deaf people assume that everything the church offers is free: an outing or a holiday – everything free. This is part of the 'Deaf psyche' discussed in chapter 9. Also it is because many Deaf people find it difficult to get a job, and will not have extra money available. Deaf people will not be embarrassed to assume things are free, or to take what is available. It is part of Deaf culture.

So you must think hard about this. Do you have the resources to offer things for free? Do you baulk at the thought? Do you feel that Deaf people should learn that someone has to pay? Do you say, 'Why should we feed them, they only come for the food?' If so, you may find that not many Deaf people come to your church at all.

This is a hard one to resolve. You may not feel able to fully give Deaf people what their culture demands. You may want to compromise, to educate and encourage. Whatever you decide to do, be assured that this hurdle will present itself.

## 14. Don't be Interpreter and Counsellor

It may be there is only one hearing person in the church who can sign, so that person interprets. But then that person is the first port of call when problems arise. That person should not attempt to be both the pastoral counsellor and interpreter. Communication is difficult enough as it is – enlist proper help. Seek a qualified member of the church. For a more serious problem, the pastor or a church officer must become involved.

Here is a true life example of what can go wrong. At a spur-of-the-moment family meeting, a deacon of a church, who was also a signer, was thrown into the twin roles of interpreter and counsellor. Tempers grew warm. He was expected to interpret back and forth and have his own input. But all his energies were focused on understanding language, and then converting, clarifying and conveying information. Also he was the referee, asking one person to stop to let another person speak, because in a heated debate people tend to speak over each other, which is impossible to interpret. When the time eventually came for him to give wise advice, his mind was scrambled and he had great difficulty. With hindsight he should have postponed the meeting, and arranged other personnel to be on hand. It is good advice to have clear demarcation from the start, and make the distinction known. Be the interpreter or the counsellor, but never both.

## 15. Trust in the Lord

There will be times when hands are weary and hearts feel cold. There will be times when patient toil is required, but there is little fruit. All the planning, toil and heartache will be for nothing without the blessing of God on your labours, but with Him there will be success. *1 Corinthians 15:58* has a wonderful promise: 'Therefore, my beloved brethren, be ye stedfast, unmoveable, always abounding in the work of the Lord, forasmuch as ye know that your labour is not in vain in the Lord.' *Isaiah 55:11* inspires us with confidence: 'So shall my word be that goeth forth out of my mouth: it shall not return unto me void, but it shall accomplish that which I please, and it shall prosper in the thing whereto I sent it.'

May the Lord bless all those who labour in this important work. Remember, the Saviour died for Deaf people also.

**Note.** Many Deaf people simply cannot understand the *Authorised* or *King James Version* of the Bible. This must be explained. The following is part of a transcript of a sermon. It is an illustration used to explain the love of the Saviour, Who will gather in all those people He has chosen. We asked a Deaf church member to read it and tell us which words he did not understand. The words are indicated here in bold: 'I remember reading the **record** of one of those men who captained a small **vessel,** taking British **troops** off at Dunkirk in the Second World War, the British **Expeditionary Force.** And I remember how he wrote that his **vessel** was **almost** full, and the **beach** was **under fire,** and the people were calling out to him, "Go, go, get away!" But the captain could see others **struggling** down the **beach, perhaps wounded** already, or **exhausted** men. And he waited and he waited, **despite** the cries of many already on **board,** until they were all on and his **vessel** was **almost overloaded.** And only then did he pull away from the danger **zone.**'

It is clear that the transcript was inaccessible, because some of the words indicated in bold are essential to the meaning of the passage, but were not understood. Indeed, some of the other words were probably misunderstood, because they are visually similar to words already in the Deaf person's vocabulary, but with sightly different spelling.

The language of Deaf people is a language of the hands. It is fluent and beautiful. It has a broad lexicon. It is equally at home with poetry, philosophy, science, current affairs and theology, to name a few. It is rich with meaning and emotion and expression. But what about Deaf people's English? For many Deaf people, English is extremely difficult to access.

Language specialists explain that the development of neurological pathways for the acquisition of language occurs mostly in the early stages of a person's life, when those pathways are open and responsive. They are stimulated by spoken or signed language. As previously mentioned most Deaf children are born to hearing families and miss this early language stimulation. Many Deaf people have never heard a word spoken, nor can recognise the sound. They are unable to recognise words, or they hear incomplete or distorted words. They may not be able to lipread words, know how they are articulated, or hear important inflection. Many have never spoken words themselves or heard their own voices saying those words. They have never heard anyone reading to them. The rules of English grammar are mysterious, with most Deaf adults reading below the level of a 9 year old. They do not use spoken English, so written English can be a minefield, fraught with misunderstandings and stumbling blocks, and may remain so despite speech and language therapy and education.

The 16th century English Bible translator William Tyndale once remarked to a Roman Catholic clergyman, 'If God spare my life ere many years, I will cause the boy that drives the plow to know more of the Scriptures than you!' He devoted his life (indeed he gave his life) to translating the Scriptures into the language of the English people. Much of his work became the King James Bible; about 90% of the New Testament is taken directly from his translation. He invented new English words and phrases, such as: mercy seat, passover, scapegoat. All this was done in an effort to give the Word of God to the ordinary farm worker. We must have that same attitude when approaching the needs of Deaf people.

English is not the first language of Deaf people. It is their second or third language. We may be guilty of keeping God's Word from Deaf people if we insist on using the King James Bible only. Clearly the aim must be an understanding of the Scriptures. In our view, the King James Bible is the starting point and the next step is a comparison with a carefully chosen easier-to-read version. The verses must be signed in BSL – the Deaf person's first language – and the text must be explained. All this takes time and patience. In a meeting for Deaf people, the reading of Scripture may entail using all the methods above. The reading will not finish until all are happy that they have understood, then the meeting can proceed. (This is one of the reasons for a dedicated meeting for Deaf people only.)

There is a vital need of glorifying God by using translations of His Holy Word that are based on trustworthy Hebrew and Greek manuscripts, executed with the greatest accuracy and faithfulness. However, there is also the practical necessity of comprehension for Deaf people. Deaf people can most certainly understand these important translation issues and be intelligently aware of the situation.

# APPENDIX

# Useful Contacts

If you want to learn about Deafness and Deaf issues, if you are looking for interpreters, if you would like to buy books and other resources, or if you want to find the nearest place to learn sign language, here is your starting point. A useful exercise is to type 'Deaf UK' into the search engine of your web browser and start to surf, or browse the links given on the following websites. Web addresses are mostly given here, because postal addresses and telephone numbers change more frequently. In alphabetical order:

**Association of Communication Support Workers:**
www.acsw.org.uk

**Association of Lipspeakers:** www.lipspeaking.co.uk

**Association of Sign Language Interpreters:** www.asli.org.uk

**British Deaf Association:** www.signcommunity.org.uk

**Council for the Advancement of Communication with Deaf People:** www.cacdp.org.uk

**Deafblind UK:** www.Deafblind.org.uk

**Forest Bookshop:** www.ForestBooks.com

**Hearing Concern:** www.hearingconcern.com

**National Association of Deafened People:** www.nadp.org.uk

**National Deaf Children's Society:** www.ndcs.org.uk

**RNID Typetalk and TextDirect:** www.typetalk.org

**Royal Association for Deaf people:** www.royalDeaf.org.uk

**Royal National Institute for Deaf people:** www.rnid.org.uk

**UK Council on Deafness (UKCoD):** www.Deafcouncil.org.uk

---

**Tabernacle Deaf Bible Fellowship**
www.MetropolitanTabernacle.org/deaf.html
The Metropolitan Tabernacle Deaf Bible Fellowship's website has a wealth of information for Deaf people – Christians and non-Christians alike. Based in London, Deaf people have travelled from as far away as Wales, Scotland, the USA, Africa, even Japan to attend meetings, and some make use of modified sermons and other resources, which are available as downloads.

**Sign Post** Local mission for Deaf and Hard of Hearing People in the Peterborough area.
Deeping Baptist Church, 42 Bridge Street, Deeping St. James, Peterborough PE6 8HA E-mail: deeping_baptist@btinternet.com
Meetings on the last Saturday of every month.

**Light of the World Mission** For Deaf people in Cardiff.
51 Dan-y-Coed Road, Cyncoed, Cardiff CF23 6ND
Tel: 029 20689283 (voice) Fax: 029 20756113

**Signs of God** An ecumenical training organisation for British Sign Language in Christian settings: www.signsofgod.org.uk

Signs of God maintain the Christian Interpreters' Network, a list of people who interpret in churches of various denominations. People on the list must hold a minimum of CACDP Stage III/NVQ Level 3 or an accepted equivalent qualification, or be Interpreters registered with CACDP or Full/Associate Members of ASLI.

# BIBLIOGRAPHY

*Interpreting: An Introduction,* Nancy Frishberg.
RID Publications (USA), ISBN 0 916883 07 08

*Interpreting Interpreting. Studies & Reflections on Sign Language Interpreting*
Frank J Harrington and Graham H Turner.
Douglas McLean, ISBN 0 946252 48 3

*The Church and Deaf People,* Roger Hitching.
Paternoster Biblical and Theological Monographs, ISBN 1 84227 222 5

*Sign Language: The Study of Deaf People and Their Language*
JG Kyle and B Woll.
Cambridge University Press, ISBN 0 521 35717 9

*The Mask of Benevolence – Disabling the Deaf Community,* Harlan Lane.
DawnSignPress, ISBN 1 58121 009 4

*When The Mind Hears – A History of the Deaf,* Harlan Lane.
Vintage Books, ISBN 0 679 72023 5

*A Beginner's Introduction to Deaf History*
Raymond Lee (Editor).
British Deaf History Society Publications, ISBN 1 902427 18 1

*Not Like Any Other Book – Interpreting the Bible,* Peter Masters.
The Wakeman Trust, ISBN 1 870855 43 4

*Sign Language Interpreting: Linguistic Coping Strategies,* Jemina Napier.
Douglas McLean, ISBN 094625 2 378

*The Linguistics of British Sign Language: An Introduction*
Rachel Sutton-Spence and Bencie Woll.
Cambridge University Press, ISBN 0 521 63718 X

*A Loss for Words,* Lou Ann Walker.
Harper Perennial, ISBN 0 06 091425 4

*Sign Language in Judaism,* Jewish Deaf Association, ISBN 0 9544841 0 X

*Deaf Perspectives: Challenging Dominant Christian Thought,*
Christian Deaf Link UK / London School of Theology.
Available at Forest Bookshop.